AILA Review

Multilingualism and minority languages:
Achievements and challenges in education

VOLUME 21 2008

Guest Editors Jasone Cenoz
Durk Gorter
University of the Basque Country / Ikerbasque

Editor Susanne Niemeier
University of Koblenz-Landau

Editorial Board Ulrich Ammon
Gerhard-Mercator-Universität, Germany
Jasone Cenoz
University of the Basque Country, Spain
Roy Lyster
McGill University
Tadhg O'hIfearnain
University of Limerick, Ireland

John Benjamins Publishing Company
Amsterdam/Philadelphia

Table of contents

Foreword

"She thinks she's great because she's good at Irish". The primary school student whose Irish fluency evoked this resentful comment from a classmate was of African origin. Her family had migrated to Ireland as refugees. The comment points to the complex identity politics that are being played out even in the early years of schooling at a time when global migration is transforming education systems in countries around the world. Whose claims to Irish identity are more legitimate — a native-born Irish student whose fluency in Irish is minimal and who resents the requirement to learn the language or a student whose family is of African origin who embraces the opportunity to learn the language? When I heard this little anecdote at a conference on migration and education in Dublin in June 2006, it reminded me of a visit I made in the mid-1970s to Scoil Bride, an all-Irish primary school (*gaelscoil*). The pride and joy of the school was a young girl of Chinese ethnic origin whose fluency in Irish surpassed most of her classmates. The nun who introduced me to this young girl was astounded both that any non-Irish person would want to learn Irish and that she had acquired the language so fluently.

These two examples highlight the centrality of *identity enhancement* as a driving force fueling students' investment in learning what the editors of this volume call *unique minority languages*. These languages have little functional utility beyond their immediate territorial zone and are seldom even required within that zone because virtually everyone is fluent in the dominant language. While external incentives or sanctions (e.g., school examinations for students or, for adults, access to jobs such as teaching that may require fluency in the language) certainly play a motivational role, sustained effort to learn the language derives primarily from the sense among learners that successful learning will enhance aspects of their identity. This enhancement of identity involves both the general sense of accomplishment that the acquisition of any form of expertise generates as well as the expanded sense of belonging that derives from linking one's own identity to the community of speakers of the language. For those whose ethnic or national origin corresponds to the language, fluency solidifies the bond to previous generations and links the individual's emerging personal narrative to the collective history of the ethnic or national group. For newcomers who aspire to be accepted and to integrate in their new homeland, access to the language stakes a claim to belonging that is difficult to ignore.

The challenge for educators lies in mobilizing students' desire to affiliate with and belong to this wider community of speakers of the minority language. Numerous factors influence the extent to which students will invest their identities in learning the

AILA Review 21 (2008), 1–3. DOI 10.1075/aila.21.01cum
ISSN 1461–0213 / E-ISSN 1570–5595 © John Benjamins Publishing Company

language. These include the health of the language at the time when revitalization efforts begin with respect to the number of speakers and the functions that the language is capable of serving within the state or region. When there are more fluent speakers, more teachers are potentially available for formal teaching of the language and informal learning can thrive within community networks.

Also of central relevance is the success with which national identity can be linked to the language, usually in opposition to past or current oppression from the dominant group. In this regard, the spectacular success of both Catalan and Basque revitalization efforts in comparison to the significant but more modest success for Frisian, Irish, and Welsh, can be attributed in part to the desire to reclaim national identities after 40 years of linguistic and social oppression under the dictatorship of General Franco. The emergence in the post-Franco era of autonomous regional governments which implemented, for the most part, enlightened language policies has clearly also played a major role.

A third factor influencing the success of language revitalization efforts concerns the success of the educational system in teaching the language. In all five contexts of unique minority language learning reviewed in this volume, the implementation of immersion and bilingual education programs in the schools has significantly increased the numbers of students from majority-language homes who have been able to develop reasonable fluency in the minority language. As documented in several of the chapters, teaching the language as a subject generally produces disappointing results in comparison to immersion or bilingual programs. If the teaching of the language is not developing expertise, then students do not experience identity enhancement. They do not experience any sense of accomplishment in acquiring fluency nor do they experience any identity bonding with the broader community of speakers of the language. Immersion and bilingual programs, by contrast, make possible identity enhancement by virtue of the fact that most students develop reasonable fluency within a relatively short period of time.

The research on immersion and bilingual education carried out since the mid-1960s demonstrated that fluency could be attained in the minority language with no adverse consequences for students' proficiency in the majority language. As this research became known to policy-makers, educators, and parents, immersion and bilingual programs expanded and have begun to produce ever-increasing numbers of fluent (albeit not necessarily grammatically accurate) speakers of the minority language.

Although the legitimacy and effectiveness of immersion and bilingual programs have been established, many issues concerning program organization and optimum instructional practices have emerged and are discussed in this volume. These issues include the extent to which a "two solitudes" model where languages are rigidly separated is preferable to a more flexible orientation that teaches for cross-lingual transfer and where the languages are brought into contact for particular purposes (e.g., creation of dual language books or projects for publication on the web). Another issue concerns the introduction of third languages: when should third languages be introduced and will this dilute the time allocation for minority and majority languages, or alternative-ly, enhance students' overall language awareness with benefits for all three languages? Finally, there is the issue of how should the home languages of migrant students be accommodated within immersion and bilingual programs. Should they be ignored on the grounds that the teachers do not speak these languages or are there ways in which they be legitimated as effective cognitive tools that serve important social and com-municative functions for the students who speak these languages?

The chapters in this volume represent a timely and significant synthesis of the knowledge base concerning minority language revitalization in the European context. Hopefully, the volume will add to the momentum of enlightened language planning that has characterized all five contexts in recent years. The expansion of more effective teaching approaches that use the minority language as a medium of instruction opens up the possibility that the challenge (and in some cases the chore) of learning minority languages can be recast as a realistic opportunity for individual and collective identity enhancement.

Jim Cummins
Toronto, October 2008

Applied Linguistics and the use of minority languages in education

Jasone Cenoz and Durk Gorter
University of the Basque Country / Ikerbasque

Why minority languages?

Minority languages can be defined is different ways. The United Nations felt a need for a clear definition of the concept 'minority' but even after many years of study was not successful in reaching full agreement. Special Rapporteur Capotorti (1979: 7) defined a minority as: "a group numerically inferior to the rest of the population of a State, in a non-dominant position, whose members — being nationals of the State — possess ethnic, religious, or characteristics differing from those of the rest of the population and show, if only implicitly, a sense of solidarity, directed towards preserving their culture, traditions, religion or language." This definition still today reflects the general understanding of minority in international law (Pentassuglia 2002: 72) and it covers most minority situations (Thompson 2001: 130). It is clear that the description given in the Charter for regional or minority languages the Council of Europe is derived from this definition. The Charter refers to "languages that are traditionally used within a given territory of a state by nationals of that state who form a group numerically smaller than the rest of the state's population and [are] different from the official language(s) of that state". However, it explicitly excludes dialects of the official language(s) of the state or the languages of migrants. From the definition is may be clear that minority does not necessarily mean 'small'. Quechua and Catalan with millions of speakers are also minority languages. The difficulty of arriving at an agreed upon definition is related to the different criteria that may be used to label a linguistic variety as a minority language or not.

Minority languages have traditionally been the concern of minority language speakers themselves and to a large extent ignored by speakers of majority languages. Minority language speakers feel minority languages as part of their identity and also very useful in everyday communication. With a few exceptions, the use of minority languages in education and research on minority languages has had a limited impact in the field of Applied Linguistics. However, there are several reasons to focus on minority languages in education and among them we could mention the following three: (i) the extended use of minority languages in the world today; (ii) the contribution of

AILA Review 21 (2008), 5–12.   DOI 10.1075/aila.21.02cen
ISSN 1461–0213 / E-ISSN 1570–5595 © John Benjamins Publishing Company

minority language speakers to multilingualism and (iii) the potential contribution of the use of minority languages in education to research in core areas of Applied Linguistics.

i) **The extended use of minority languages in the world today**. Nowadays there are an estimated 5,000 to 7,000 languages in the world. It is difficult to know the exact number of languages because the distinction between a language and a dialect is not always clear. The Ethnologue (Gordon, 2005) considers that there are 6,912 languages in the world today, but some of the languages included are just considered varieties or dialects in other accounts. Africa and Asia have a much larger number of languages than other parts of the world. The number of speakers of the different languages can be one of the indicators to estimate the spread of minority languages. In fact, according to the Ethnologue, 40 percent of the world's population have one of the most common eight languages as a first language. These languages are Mandarin, Hindi, Spanish, English, Bengali, Portuguese, Arabic and Russian. The data in the Ethnologue also indicate that over 350 million people in the world (6.1% of the world's population) speak languages with less than one million speakers. It is likely that many of these speakers of 'smaller' languages are speakers of minority languages. These figures are quite important to be taken into consideration in the study of APPLIED LINGUISTICS. Another indicator of the demographic extent of minority languages is the fact that all the languages in the world are spoken in a very limited number of states (about 200) and governments of many countries give official recognition to only one or some of the languages spoken in the country or in part of the country. In fact, it would be difficult to find a country which is completely monolingual because multilingualism is the rule not the exception (see Edwards, 1994; Romaine, 2000). When several languages are spoken in the same state there are usually important asymmetries regarding their demography, status and legal support. Some languages can be demographically relatively strong but still share some of the characteristics of minority languages; again Quechua and Catalan would be good examples.

ii) **The contribution of minority language speakers to multilingualism**. Most of the population in western cultures in Europe and North America are monolingual in one of the 'big' languages and only exposed to other languages in the school context or through the media. This is not the case in many other parts of the world where a very large number of languages is spoken as for example in Papua New Guinea, Indonesia, Nigeria or India. Being monolingual is also exceptional in the case of speakers of minority languages. Even in Western Europe, speakers of minority languages such as Basque, Catalan, Frisian, Irish and Welsh need to be multilingual. They all speak at least the majority languages they are in contact with (Spanish, French, Dutch or English). In many cases, when neither the minority nor the majority language is English they need to have some command of English as an additional language for international contacts, for travel or for using the internet. Minority language speakers are at least bilingual and learn additional languages at school.

iii) **The potential contribution of the use of minority languages in education to research in core areas of Applied Linguistics.** The acquisition, teaching and learning of minority languages and research analysing these processes is linked to many core areas in applied linguistics. These areas include L1 literacy, second language acquisition, bilingualism and multilingualism, language and identity, language policy, and the acquisition of additional languages. There are some specific issues that are distinctive for minority languages but at the same time situations involving the teaching and learning of minority languages share many of the challenges of teaching and learning languages of high status or languages of wider communication. Traditionally there has been a complete separation between international bi/multilingual schools and the so-called *'elite bilingualism'* teaching languages such as English, German or French and the so-called *'folk bilingual education'* for minority language populations. This volume contributes to establishing links between the two situations by focusing on minority *'folk-bilingual education'* but in situations where the speakers of these minority languages are not economically disadvantaged compared to majority language speakers. The analysis of the experience and research conducted in these settings can have implications not only for all types of bi/multilingual education but also for language learning and language acquisition in other educational settings that are not usually labelled as bilingual or multilingual.

Minority languages in Western Europe

The multifarious constellation of languages of Europe comprises a range of minority languages in Western Europe. The 47 member states of the Council of Europe have 41 languages as official state languages. The figure includes the 27 member states of the European Union which share 23 official languages. However, because minorities are defined by their relation to the state, the number of minority languages in the geographic territory of Europe is much larger. Different categories of minority languages can be distinguished (Extra and Gorter 2008: 24–28). Many languages are a minority in one state but the official and dominant language in another, neighbouring state. These language groups with a 'kin-state' may share having the status of being a minority, but the linguistic relationship between the dominated and dominant language differs from case to case. Multiple cases of such language groups are, for instance, Albanian in Italy and Greece; Croatian in Italy and Austria or German in Belgium, Czech Republic, Denmark, France, Italy, Poland and Denmark.

The other important category are so-called 'unique' minority languages, which are spoken in one or sometimes more than one state, but are nowhere the official dominant or majority language of a state. These minorities show a lot of variation. They may be extremely small and on the verge of extinction such as Livonian in Latvia or Ume Sami in Sweden, where the youngest speakers are over 60 years of age. But the category also comprises language groups that have obtained official status, a fair degree of political and economic support and strong favourable attitudes by their speakers in order to revitalise them and give these languages a sustainable future.

In a final category we find a few languages that are official state languages, but in practice function in sociological and economic terms largely in the same way as other minority languages. They are dominated by one or more other majority languages, such as in the case of Luxembourgish, which is official in Luxembourg but has to compete with French and German, or Irish which is the first official language of the Irish Republic, but is dominated to a large extent by English.

This volume discusses the educational contexts and research conducted on five minority languages in Western Europe: Basque, Catalan, Irish, Welsh and Frisian. These situations share some common characteristics:

- They are spoken in countries that are part of the European Union: Spain, France, Ireland, United Kingdom and the Netherlands;
- They are autochthonous languages, because they originate from the areas where they are still spoken today;
- They are languages that are in contact with a 'stronger' language and all speakers of the minority language are also fluent in the national language, which is also part of the school curriculum;
- They are 'unique' in the sense of not being spoken in other countries as a majority language.

The five situations discussed in this volume also have some challenges in common with other situations involving minority languages or even languages which are demographically strong but do not have a strong tradition of being used as languages of instruction in education. These challenges are:

- The use of a standard language in education. The five situations have already made a lot of progress in the standardization of the languages but the standardization of the language or the variety to be used in education and other contexts such as the media or institutions has been a major challenge in the past.
- Legal status and funding. The five minority languages discussed in this volume have legal support and funding to be used in education even if there are important differences when comparing the languages or the areas where some of these languages are used. Some of these languages have had important legal problems to be recognized in the past and as a consequence financial problems.
- Development of teaching material. Minority languages face more problems than majority languages in the production of educational materials. The obvious reason for this is that materials are published for a more limited market but in most cases minority languages also face the problem of having a weak tradition in the use of academic language. In many cases the production of specialized books goes along with the publications of specialized dictionaries. The different situations discussed here are at different stages in the production of teaching material.

- Availability of qualified teachers. This is a challenge for the use of minority languages in education because there are fewer qualified teachers with a good command of a minority language than of a majority language. In some situations it may also be difficult to get specialized training to teach some specific minority languages or to teach through these languages. Regarding this issue, there are differences between the situations in this volume.
- New challenges in modern society. All the educational contexts discussed in this volume face new challenges in society derived from the immigration of speakers of other languages, from new ways of communication and the development of new technologies. The effects of mass-tourism and globalisation can be added to these challenges. These changes are sometimes felt as threatening for minority languages.

The five situations involving Basque, Catalan, Welsh, Irish and Frisian also have some important differences:

- The five minority languages involved do not have the same linguistic origin. Four of the five languages are Indo-European but belong to different families. Welsh and Irish are Celtic languages, Frisian is a Germanic language, and Catalan is a Romance language. Basque is a non-Indo-European language of unknown origin.
- The linguistic distance between the minority language and the majority language(s) is not the same. Welsh and Irish are very different from English, the majority language they are in contact with. Basque is also very different from Spanish and French, the Romance languages it is in contact with. Frisian is linguistically close to Dutch, both being Germanic languages. Catalan is a Romance language that is related to the other Romance languages (Spanish, French, Sardinian and Italian) that is has contacts with.
- There are very important differences in demography. The number of speakers may be hard to establish, because it depends on the criteria of what counts as a language speaker and on the method of measurement. Most certainly Catalan has by far most speakers, estimated up to 9 million. Basque and Welsh have over 600,000 speakers each and Frisian around 400,000. For Irish 1,66 million people have reported themselves as competent speakers in the 2006 census, but only 40 percent actually uses the language.
- There are also very important differences in the degree of official protection and promotion of these languages. Irish is the first national language in Ireland and has the status as one of the 23 official languages of the European Union. Basque and Catalan are co-official languages (along with Spanish) in parts of Spain but their legal status is much weaker in France. Welsh has some rights derived from the Welsh Language Act of 1993 which put Welsh on equal footing with English in Wales, but there is a campaign for a new act to give it full official status. Frisian has obtained some official recognition as a 'second language of the Kingdom of the Netherlands'.

–   The European Charter for Regional or Minority Languages has been signed and ratified by the states of Spain, the Netherlands and the United Kingdom, whereby different degrees of protection were promised according to this European standard. For Basque and Catalan it added little to the level of promotion offered already by the regional governments and for Welsh most provisions of the Charter were also in force already. For Frisian the ratification and monitoring of the Charter has implied important moral support, although less has changed in practice. The state of Ireland has refused from the beginning to sign the Charter out of fear of reduction of the existing measures to promote Irish.

–   All these minority languages are used in education but the extent to which they are used as the main language of instruction varies considerably. Basque and Catalan have become the main languages of instruction in the Basque Autonomous Community and in Catalonia but their use is not as strong in other areas where Basque or Catalan is spoken. The use of Welsh as the medium of instruction has substantially increased over the last decades. On the other hand, the development of Irish in education shows points of weakening and at the same time strengthening of all Irish schools. The position of Frisian in education is the weakest of these five cases and overall there are not many changes going on.

–   Another difference between the situations is the use of English. In the case of Welsh and Irish, English is the dominant language which the minority language is in contact with but in the other three situations English is a third language in the school curriculum. There are also important differences between the more extensive use of English in society in Friesland and the more limited use of English in Catalonia or the Basque Country.

Research on minority languages

Research on minority languages is ordinarily not well known by speakers of 'big' languages but it has focused on several areas of Applied Linguistics and it is relevant to many areas. The situations discussed in this volume include research on the acquisition of minority languages as a first language and as a second language by speakers of majority languages. They also refer to situations of bilingual and multilingual education involving the use of minority, majority and even foreign languages as languages of instruction. These situations also refer to the spread of content based instruction as an effective approach in language teaching in educational settings. Minority languages in education can also be of interest to researchers working on language policy and language planning or language assessment.

Each of the articles emphasizes some aspects of research, depending on the recent developments in each case and on the availability of specific types of research results.

In the first article, *"Achievements and challenges in bilingual and multilingual education in the Basque Country"* Jasone Cenoz summarizes the results of different educational linguistic models in the Basque Autonomous Community regarding achievement in Basque, Spanish, English and other school subjects. She also discusses the new challenges for the Basque educational system which include the need for more effective teaching of languages of wider communication and the integration of immigrant students.

F. Xavier Vila i Moreno discusses the situation of Catalan in *"Language-in-education policies in the Catalan language area"*. He provides an overview of the main school models in the fragmented Catalan language area from a comparative perspective. His summary of recent research results emphasizes language learning, language practices, effects on social cohesion and academic achievement. The challenges of the education systems are to adapt to a new multilingual, multicultural environment, where immigrant languages combine with globalization. At the same time, these systems may be regarded with suspicion by majority speakers, especially those who live in traditionally monolingual areas.

The next article by John Harris *"The declining role of primary schools in the revitalisation of Irish"* focuses on the major challenge of the education system in Ireland which has to constantly produce a high proportion of people with good Irish in order to maintain the small proportion of Irish-speaking households. He examines evidence from national surveys of pupil achievement and attitudes in order to establish how well this strategy is working. Results show a long-term decline in success in learning Irish in mainstream schools and to a lesser extent in Gaeltacht schools.

The situation in Wales is discussed by W. Gwyn Lewis in *"Current Challenges in bilingual Education in Wales"*. He commences with a brief summary of the development and current statistics on bilingual education in Wales. He then discusses the inadequacies of current typologies and terminology in bilingual education models. The early results from a 2007/08 survey of language allocation in bilingual schools in Wales are presented, along with an emerging new typology. He points out that if Welsh-medium and bilingual education is to flourish in the twenty first century, it must do so in accordance with the needs and aspirations of the children and parents.

In the fifth case study in this volume Durk Gorter and Cor van der Meer discuss *"Developments in bilingual Frisian-Dutch education in Friesland"*. They give an outline of the weak position of Frisian in the education system and the slow development of language policy. They discuss the research outcomes on language attitudes, school achievement in Dutch and Frisian and an experiment with a number of trilingual schools. Although the general point of departure for Frisian is encouraging, the way Frisian is taught in the schools reflects the position of Frisian as a predominantly spoken language in society at large.

These five situations focus on the achievements and challenges faced by minority languages in education in some countries in Europe but we strongly believe that they are relevant for applied linguists all over the world.

References

Capotorti, F. 1979. *Study on the Rights of Persons Belonging to Ethnic, Religious and Linguistic Minorities.* New York NY: United Nations. UN Doc.E/CN.4/Suh.2/384/Rev.1.

European Charter for Regional or Minority Languages. 1998. Strasbourg: Council of Europe.

Edwards, J. 1994. *Multilingualism.* London: Routledge.

Extra, G. & Gorter, D. 2008. The constellation of languages in Europe: An inclusive approach. In *Multilingual Europe: Facts and Policies,* G. Extra & D. Gorter (eds), 3–60. Berlin: Mouton de Gruyter.

Gordon, R.G., Jr. (ed.). 2005. *Ethnologue: Languages of the World,* 15th edn. Dallas TX: SIL International. Online version: http://www.ethnologue.com/. [Accessed 20.10.2008].

Pentassuglia, G. 2002. *Minorities in International Law: An Introductory Study.* Strasbourg: Council of Europe Publishing.

Romaine, S. 2000. Multilingualism. In *The Handbook of Linguistics,* M. Aronoff & J. Rees-Miller (eds), 512–532. Oxford: Blackwell.

Thompson, C. 2001. The protection of minorities within the United Nations. In *Minority Rights in Europe,* S.Trifunovska (ed.), 115–138. The Hague: Asser Press.

Author's addresses

Jasone Cenoz
Department of Research Methods in
Education, FICE
University of the Basque Country
Tolosa Hiribidea 70
20018 San Sebastian, Spain

jasone.cenoz@ehu.es

Durk Gorter
University of the Basque Country/Ikerbasque
FICE
Tolosa Hiribidea 70
20018 San Sebastian-Spain

d.gorter@ikerbasque.org

Achievements and challenges in bilingual and multilingual education in the Basque Country

Jasone Cenoz
University of the Basque Country

This paper focuses on the use of Basque as the language of instruction. In the first part of the article the situation of Basque in the Basque Country is briefly described and the different possibilities regarding the language(s) of instruction are explained: model A with Spanish as the language of instruction and Basque as a subject; model B with both Basque and Spanish as languages of instruction and model D with Basque as the language of instruction and Spanish as a subject. Then, the results of research studies comparing these three models regarding achievement in Basque, Spanish and other areas of the curriculum are analysed. Finally the article considers the new challenges the Basque educational system is facing. One of these challenges is the need to go from bilingual education to multilingual education by teaching in a more effective way languages of wider communication. Another recent challenge is multiculturalism as a response to the increasing immigrant population which is a new phenomenon in the Basque educational system. The need for a more holistic approach towards multilingualism both in teaching and research is proposed so as to face these new challenges.

The Basque Country and Basque

The Basque Country spreads along the Bay of Biscay, north and south of the Pyrenees in France and Spain. The Basque Country comprises seven provinces, three belong to the French department 'Pyrénées Atlantiques'(Iparraldea) and the other four provinces to two autonomous regions in Spain (the Basque Autonomous Community and Navarre). The total population of the Basque Country is approximately three million and the most populated area is the Basque Autonomous Community (BAC) in Spain with over two million inhabitants.

Basque is completely different from French and Spanish and is the only non-Indoeuropean language in Western Europe. French and Spanish are Romance languages and Basque is a language whose origin is unknown. This can clearly be seen when

AILA Review 21 (2008), 13–30. DOI 10.1075/aila.21.03cen
ISSN 1461–0213 / E-ISSN 1570–5595 © John Benjamins Publishing Company

we comparing the translation of the sentence '*Do you work here?*' in the following example:

> French: *Tu travailles ici?*
> Spanish: *¿Tu trabajas aquí?*
> Basque: *Hemen lan egiten duzu?*

Basque is a minority language which has miraculously survived in contact with two strong languages. It was widely spoken in most parts of the Basque Country and even in neighbouring areas in the Middle Ages but since then the territory where Basque is spoken has shrank as the result of contact with Romance languages. The Basque language, which did not have a strong written tradition, suffered an important retreat in the last three centuries and mainly in the twentieth century. Some of the factors that have made the Basque language weaker are political such as the the 'Spanish only' policy during Franco's dictatorship (1939–1975), but they also include industrialization and the development of communications and the mass media (see also Azurmendi & Martínez de Luna 2005; Cenoz, 2008a).

Nowadays Basque has approximately 800,000 speakers but practically all of them are also fluent in either French or Spanish. Basque is a minority all over the Basque Country and Spanish and French are the main languages also in the cities (Bilbao, Donostia-San Sebastian, Vitoria-Gasteiz, Biarritz, Bayonne, etc). Basque is used more often than Spanish or French in everyday communication only in some limited areas of the Basque Country.

According to the most recent sociolinguistic survey conducted by the Basque Government (Basque Government, 2008) there are important differences in the knowledge of Basque when the different areas are compared. In the following table we can see the percentages corresponding to the knowledge of Basque in the BAC, Navarre and Iparraldea according to the most recent survey.

Table 1. Knowledge of Basque in the Basque Country

	BAC	Navarre	Iparraldea
Proficient in Basque	30.1%	11.1%	22.5%
Passive skills in Basque	18.3%	7.6%	8.6%
No knowledge of Basque	51.5%	81.3%	68.9%

Source: IV Inkesta Soziolinguistikoa, Basque Government, 2008

The data indicate that the BAC is the area where proficiency in Basque is higher and Navarre is the area with the lowest proficiency. Most passive bilinguals, who can understand Basque but have limited production skills, live in the BAC. The data also indicate that even in the BAC more than half of the population over 16 cannot use or understand Basque.

There are importance differences in legislation regarding the status of Basque in the three different areas: the BAC, Navarre and Iparraldea. Political and social changes in Spain have allowed for the possibility of establishing a strong language policy to support and develop the use of Basque. The Spanish Constitution (1978) declared Spanish the nationwide official language and guaranteed the rights of Spanish speakers to use their language but also raised the possibility of recognizing other languages as co-official in their own territories. Legal recognition can have important implications for the resources allocated to the development of Basque and therefore for its maintenance and revival. Nowadays, Basque has a co-official status in the BAC and there is a strong policy to protect and develop the Basque language. Basque is also official in the Northern area of Navarre where the Basque Language Law (1986) establishes a linguistic zoning that divides the community into three parts (see Oroz & Sotés, 2008). The status of Basque is much weaker in Iparraldea, in France. The effect of language policy can clearly be seen when looking at the development of the number of speakers of Basque over the last years (Basque Government, 2008).

Table 2. Development of proficiency in Basque (over 16 years old)

	1991	1996	2001	2006
BAC	24.1	27.7	29.4	30.1
Navarre	9.5	9.6	10.3	11.1
Iparraldea	–	26.4	24.8	22.5

Source: IV Inkesta Soziolinguistikoa, Basque Government, 2008

When looking at the development of proficiency in Basque along the years we can see that the number of Basque speakers is increasing in the BAC and there is also a slight increase in Navarre. However the percentage of speakers in Iparraldea, where the policy to protect Basque is extremely weak, is decreasing.

The use of Basque in education

Bilingual education is not a recent phenomenon in the Basque Country. Some schools in the BAC were bilingual or even trilingual (in Basque, Spanish, and French) at the end of the nineteenth century. However, the use of Basque was banned from education during the Franco regime (1939–1975). Despite legal strictures, in the 1960s, groups of enthusiastic parents and teachers fought for and succeeded in re-opening a number of private Basque-medium schools. These schools were not officially recognized in the beginning, but they were finally accepted because they had attracted so many students that they could not be ignored. Some years later, Basque, along with Spanish, was recognized as an official language in the BAC by the law on the Normalization of the Basque Language (1982) and three models of language schooling were established (models A, B and D). The use of Basque in education is more common in the BAC than in Navarre or Iparraldea. The rest of this article will focus mainly on the BAC.

A model schools are intended for native speakers of Spanish who choose to be instructed in Spanish. Basque is taught as a second language for 4 to 5 hours a week. These schools provide minimal instruction and, thus, minimal proficiency in Basque as a second language. Basque is learned as a second language and most of these schools are located in areas where Basque is used much less than Spanish so pupils do not need Basque for daily communication. This type of school is similar to many schools in many parts of the world where second and foreign languages are learned only in the classroom.

B model schools are intended for native speakers of Spanish who want to be bilingual in Basque and Spanish. With this aim in mind, both Basque and Spanish are used as languages of instruction for approximately 50% of school time, although there is considerable variation from school to school (Arzamendi & Genesee, 1997). Basque is the second language for all children in this model and it is not only a school subject but also the medium of instruction for other subjects. This model has some similarities with Canadian immersion models in which French and English are used as languages of instruction for majority group English-speaking students (Genesee, 1987). In both cases, pupils who are speakers of the majority have their L1 and an L2 as the medium of instruction. The B model is closer to partial immersion but the target language is a language of wider communication in the case of Canadian immersion and a minority language, in the case of the Basque Country. The use of a second language as the language of instruction for some subjects can also be found in many international schools all over the world (De Mejia, 2002; Carder, 2007). However, in the case of international schools languages of wider communication and not minority languages are used as medium of instruction. Situations which are closer to the B model can be found in other minority situations described in the other articles of this volume.

D model schools were originally created as a language maintenance program for native speakers of Basque. Basque is the language of instruction and Spanish is taught as a subject for 4 to 5 hours a week. The original idea was to give pupils with Basque as their L1 the opportunity to have their own minority languages as the language of instruction.

However, this model currently also includes a large number of students with Spanish as their first language. There are many possible reasons for Spanish-speaking parents to choose the D model. In some cases the language was lost in the family and parents are in favour of recovering Basque. Other parents feel that as they live in the Basque Country, it is a good idea for their children to learn Basque now that there is an opportunity to do so. There are also practical reasons to learn Basque as it is a requirement in some jobs. The fact is that an increasing number of Spanish L1 pupils have Basque as the language of instruction. The percentages vary depending on the area where the school is located. In some schools, most pupils speak Spanish at home and in others there are more pupils with Basque than Spanish as their first language. The situation in model D is interesting because of the mixture of both linguistic backgrounds. Consequently, Model D schools can be regarded as a very intense type of total immersion program for native Spanish-speaking students and a first language

Table 3. Percentages of pupils in the different models in primary and compulsory secondary education in the BAC 2008–2009 (public and private schools)[a]

	A Spanish	B (B & S)	D Basque
Primary (6–12)	8.80%	29.96%	60.47%
Compulsory secondary (12–16)	19.08%	27.54%	52.64%

Source: Basque Government Department of Education (www.hezkuntza.net)
[a] The percentages do not add up to 100% because a very limited number of students who are in the BAC for a short period do not study Basque

maintenance program for native Basque speakers. The distribution of students in the different models can be seen in Table 3.

The data indicate that the use of Basque as the language of instruction attracts most students. Model D with Basque as the language of instruction is the most popular followed by model B. Basque is more commonly used as the language of instruction in the lower levels of education. That means that the use of Basque as the language of instruction in secondary school is likely to increase in the future when these children get older. The distribution is not the same in different areas of the BAC but the trend to use more Basque as the language of instruction has taken place in all three provinces of the BAC (Araba, Bizkaia and Gipuzkoa).

Teaching through the medium of Basque has also increased in Navarre but it is more limited. Navarre is divided into three linguistic zones and Basque is the language of instruction for 88.12% of the students in the Bascophone zone, 30,13% in the mixed zone and 5.9% in the non-Bascophone zone (see Oroz & Sotés, 2008). The use of Basque as the language of instruction in the whole of Navarre is 26.28% because the Bascophone zone is less populated than the other two zones. The use of Basque as the language of instruction in Iparraldea is more modest and Basque is the language of instruction for less than 10% of the students (see Azurmendi, Larrañaga & Apalategi, 2008).

Just over 50% of school children in the BAC attend private schools (Basque Government Department of Education, 2008). These schools have very strong funding from the Basque Government but parents still have to pay a fee and this implies that there can be differences in socioeconomic background between public and private schools. The use of Basque as the language of instruction is very popular in both types of school but even more common in the public than in the private schools.

There has been a dramatic increase in the use of Basque as the language of instruction in the last 25 years if we take into account that only 20% of students had Basque-medium teaching (model B and D) when the models were established in 1982 (see also Zalbide & Cenoz, 2008). Parents can choose the model they want for their children, and each model is available in the public and private sectors but access to all three options is limited in some areas where there are not enough students interested in a particular model. One of the characteristics of the Basque-medium education is its spread in contrast to many other projects of immersion and minority language instruction which are not available for the whole population of a specific area.

The increase in the use of Basque as the language of instruction has had important implications for the educational system. Zalbide & Cenoz (2008) point out that important changes have taken place in the teachers' proficiency in Basque and the development of teaching and learning materials in Basque. However, the success of using the minority language as the main language of instruction does not necessarily imply that students use it in everyday communication.

The outcomes of bilingual education

There have been a large number of research studies and evaluations of bilingual education in the BAC in the last 25 years. These studies have used different methodological approaches but most of them have analysed the linguistic and non-linguistic results of teaching through the medium of Basque, Spanish or both languages (see Cenoz 2008b). This is a major concern when there has been a major shift in the medium of instruction and also when Basque is the medium of instruction not only for native speakers of Basque but also for learners with Basque as a second language. An additional concern that is not shared by languages of wider communication is related to the fact that Basque is a minority language. Nowadays that Basque is the main language of instruction '*Can you teach mathematics through Basque?*' is no longer common in the Basque Country but it was often asked in the past when Basque did not have a strong tradition of being used in academic contexts. In this section, we are going to summarize the outcomes of bilingual education in the BAC by looking at proficiency in Basque, proficiency in Spanish and other areas of the curriculum. In order to illustrate these outcomes the results of a specific study will be given as an example of the general trend found in most evaluations of bilingual education conducted in the BAC. The examples given come from an evaluation of the last year of primary school conducted by the *Basque Institute for Research and Evaluation in Education* (ISEI-IVEI). Participants were 2053 pupils aged 11 and 12 and the comparisons include not only the three different models but also the type of school, that is, whether the school is public or private (see ISEI-IVEI, 2006).

Proficiency in Basque. Several studies have focused on achievement in Basque across the models. The general finding is that there are significant differences in Basque proficiency when the three models are compared. Students in Model D are more proficient in Basque than students in Model B who, in turn, are more proficient than students in Model A (see Cenoz, forthcoming for a review). These are the most remarkable differences between the models. The ISEI-IVEI evaluation at the end of primary school measured listening, reading, writing, dictation, grammar and lexis. The mean obtained by the sample in the total score for Basque was 250 (range from 150 to 350). The distribution of the scores in the different models in public and private schools can be seen in Figure 1.

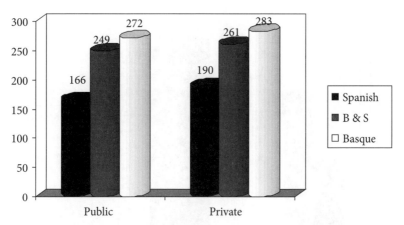

Figure 1. Basque proficiency in the last year of primary education (IVEI-ISEI, 2006)

The results indicate that the language of instruction has an important effect on Basque proficiency both in the public and private networks. The best results are obtained by students with Basque as the only language of instruction and they are followed by those in the B model with Basque and Spanish as the languages of instruction and the lowest are found in the A model. These results are not a surprise not only because more hours of exposure can have an effect on proficiency but also because model D includes students with Basque as their first language.

Proficiency in Spanish. When studies have analysed proficiency in Spanish across the models, the general finding has been that there are no important differences. In contrast to the findings on Basque proficiency, the language of instruction does not have a significant effect on proficiency in Spanish (see Cenoz, forthcoming for a review of these studies). The main reason for this lack of influence seems to be related to the dominant position of Spanish in society. In fact, even students with Basque as their first language who study through the medium of Basque are exposed to Spanish in different ways. In many cases they are in close contact with students who speak Spanish at home but they are also exposed to Spanish in the media and in many cases in everyday interaction with people who do not speak Basque. Students with Basque as the language of instruction study Spanish at school as a subject but Spanish is taught in the same way as for students who have Spanish as a first language and Spanish as the language of instruction. The ISEI-IVEI evaluation at the end of primary school measured listening, reading and writing. The mean obtained by the sample in the total score for Spanish was 258,2 (range from 150 to 350). The distribution of the scores in the different models in public and private schools can be seen in Figure 2.

The results do not show a clear effect of the language of instruction on proficiency in Spanish. In fact, the highest and the lowest scores can be found in the A model where Spanish is the language of instruction. The results indicate that the differences that could be related to the socioeconomic status (public and private schools) seem to

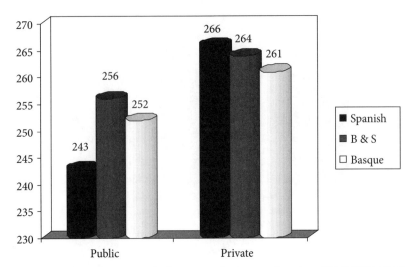

Figure 2. Spanish proficiency in the last year of primary education (IVEI-ISEI, 2006)

be more important than the language of instruction. Only in the case of the private schools, more exposure to Spanish seems to be related to the results but the D model in the private network obtains higher results than the A and B models in the public network.

Other areas of the curriculum. Another important question when looking at the outcomes of bilingual education is to see whether there are differences in academic development in other areas. Evaluations of achievement in mathematics and the natural and social sciences indicate that the differences between the networks (public vs. private) are more important than the differences between the models (see Cenoz, forthcoming) An example of this trend can be found in the same evaluation of the last year of primary school in the case of mathematics. The results are given in Figure 3.

The results indicate that private schools do better than public schools in general and that the main differences are between the public and the private schools in the case of the A model. Once again the socioeconomic factors seem to be more important than the language of instruction. These differences between the networks have also been found in the PISA evaluations conducted in secondary schools of the BAC (ISEI-IVEI, 2008). The aim of the Pisa assessments is to develop indicators so as to compare the participating countries in subjects such as mathematics, science and literacy skills (http://www.pisa.oecd.org). The 2006 PISA assessment was signed up by 57 countries including Spain and there was a separate sample for the BAC. The were no differences between the results in the BAC and the average for the OECD in any of the subjects but the results in the BAC were significantly higher than the average results in Spain.

Another area that has received a lot of attention by researchers is the evaluation of results in English. A first foreign language is compulsory and a second foreign language is an optional subject in Basque schools in the BAC (Cenoz, 2005). Most students have

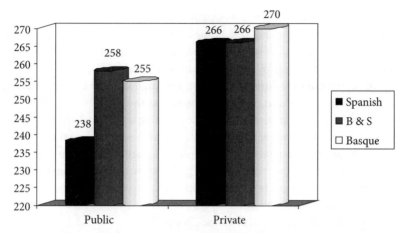

Figure 3. Mathematics in the last year of primary education (IVEI-ISEI, 2006)

English as their first foreign language and French is very popular for those students who choose to study a second foreign language in secondary school. Some research studies have compared different models and have reported that students who have Basque as the language of instruction obtain better scores in English than students instructed through Spanish, the majority language (Cenoz, 1992; Lasagabaster, 1998; Sagasta, 2003). This effect could be observed even when variables such as general intelligence, motivation, SES and contact with English outside school were controlled (see Cenoz & Valencia, 1994).

In sum, results from evaluations of bilingual schools in the BAC indicate that using a minority language as the language of instruction results in better proficiency in the minority and similar levels of achievement in the majority language and other subjects such as mathematics. Higher proficiency in the minority language in the context of the BAC is equivalent to more balanced bilingualism because of the extended knowledge of Spanish. This knowledge of two languages gives some advantages when acquiring English as a third language. This effect can be explained as related to a higher development of metalinguistic awareness or learning strategies and it can also be linked to the fact that bilinguals have a wider linguistic repertoire that can be used as a basis in third language acquisition (see also Cenoz, 2003).

In the case of Spanish-speaking children who are instructed through the medium of Basque in the B and D models, these results corroborate results obtained in Canadian immersion programs (see for example Genesee, 1987). They show that when the first language is the majority language and has enough opportunities for development, it is possible to use another language as the language of instruction. Using a second or foreign language as the medium of instruction is considered a very positive experience in the case of international and European schools (Baetens Beardsmore, 1997; Carder, 2007). In all these situations, students achieve a high level of proficiency in the second language at no cost of their first language proficiency or academic development.

At the same time, the results of evaluations carried out in the BAC indicate that instruction through the first language in the case of native speakers of an indigenous minority language can be successful for their linguistic and academic development.

Using Basque as the language of instruction gives students with Basque as a home language the opportunity to develop their own language and at the same time Spanish lessons allow them to acquire the formal aspects of the majority language in society. This situation is in clear contrast with the situation in the past when Basque was banned from school and Basque speakers were taught through the medium of Spanish and did not acquire literacy skills in their own language. Apart from the situations described in this volume, there are many examples of successful teaching through indigenous minority languages in different parts of the world. Some examples can be found in Hawaii, Arizona, New Zealand and Latin America (see McCarty, Romero & Zepeda, 2006; López & Sichra, 2007; Hamel, 2007).

The A model has the students' first language as the language of instruction and Basque as a subject so it cannot be regarded as bilingual education but just as second language teaching. This model has very different results in the public and private networks and this has been related to socioeconomic status because the A model in the public network has more students than the other models from lower socioeconomic backgrounds. This factor is indeed more important than the language of instruction when analysing the linguistic and non-linguistic outcomes of bilingual education.

The challenges of teaching through a minority language

Using a minority language as the language of instruction faces many challenges. Some challenges are specific for minority languages, others are common in many other situations where a second or foreign language is used as the medium of instruction. In this section we will look at different types of challenges faced by Basque-medium teaching.

A first challenge for minority languages in education is legal recognition and funding. Basque has had dark times but nowadays it has a privileged position in the BAC as compared to many minorities around the world. It is a co-official language, it is part of the curriculum and it can be used as the language of instruction in models B and D. The situation in Navarre and Iparraldea is not as strong legally as it is in the BAC (see Oroz & Sotés, 2008). Spain signed The Charter for Regional or Minority Languages in 1992 and ratified it in 2001 but France has not signed the Charter yet (Council of Europe, 2008).

Another challenge which is shared with many other minority languages is the use of a standard variety of the language at school. Many minority languages, including Basque, have a relatively poor writing tradition as compared to languages of wider communication and they have not been used to a large extent as languages of instructions or at the institutional level. This situation has not favoured the development of a standard. These factors together with the low social prestige of the language and the geographical characteristics of the Basque Country can explain the existence of different Basque dialects in a small territory. The Academy of the Basque Language (Euskaltzaindia), founded in 1918, defined a unified standard variety of Basque called 'euskara batua' (unified Basque) in the 60's. This standard variety is the most widespread variety of Basque and is generally used in official documents, the mass media (Basque television, radios and newspapers) and in literature. 'Euskara batua' is also the variety used at school, in educational materials and in the teaching of Basque as a second language. Nowadays, many teachers use other varieties orally but textbooks are usually in 'batua'. The dispute about the variety to be used in education is not nowadays at the forefront because of its extended use.

Basque and other minority languages discussed in this volume also face the challenge of language use. Schools can be quite successful in teaching the minority language and encouraging its use at school but the use of minority languages as languages of instruction does not automatically imply that they are used in every conversation. In a way, the limited use outside the classroom also happens in the case of foreign language teaching but there are some differences between the two situations. Even if exposure to the target language outside school is similar and very limited in both cases, languages of wider communication taught as foreign languages are languages with millions of native and non-native speakers. In contrast, minority languages such as Basque, and the other languages discussed in this volume are only spoken as minority languages and if future generations do not use them they may just die out.

The 2006 survey of the Basque language shows that 25% of the population in the whole of the Basque Country uses Basque but only 9.9% uses more Basque than Spanish or French (Basque Government, 2008). Many speakers, including students, are proficient in Basque but they find it easier to use their first language, Spanish or French. Proficiency in a specific language is a necessary first step to use it but it does not mean that Spanish or French speakers are going to shift from using their first language to a second language for all purposes in everyday life. Some Spanish speakers have made a big effort to shift to Basque as a home language but many others only use Basque in some situations. The sociolinguistic context can also have a very important influence in language use. It is common for schoolchildren in Spanish-speaking areas to use Spanish among each other but Basque with the teacher even in the D model. There are special language policy plans for schools to promote the use of Basque (Aldekoa & Gardner, 2002; Zalbide & Cenoz, 2008) but the minority status of Basque in society cannot be completely counterbalanced by the work done by schools.

An additional challenge faced by minority languages is related to language attitudes. Developing positive attitudes towards language learning can be desirable in any context of second or foreign language learning but there are differences between learning a language of wider communication and a minority language because in the latter case it is also possible to communicate in the majority language. Learning and speaking Basque is considered an essential part of Basque identity by many speakers but some learners do not find it useful (see see Azurmendi, Larrañaga & Apalategi,

2008 about identity). Some studies have reported differences in attitudes between the models. For example Aiestaran (2003) found that the attitudes of students in the B and D models in the non-Basque speaking area of Rioja Alavesa in the BAC were more positive than the attitudes of A model students.

Cenoz (2002) compared attitudes towards Basque, Spanish and English in primary and secondary school in a Basque-medium school in an area where Basque is spoken by 54% of the population. She found that language attitudes were more positive in primary than in secondary school but also that attitudes towards Basque were more positive than attitudes towards the other two languages. These results indicate that the level of proficiency, the school model and the sociolinguistic context can influence attitudes towards learning and using the majority language.

Some of the challenges faced by Basque and other minority languages are also found in many school situations in which a new language is used as the medium of instruction. One of these challenges is to have enough teachers who are proficient enough to teach through the medium of the target language. Nowadays approximately 90% of the teachers in the public network and 63% in the private network are fluent in Basque and hold the required certificate. Many of these teachers have learned Basque as a second language in adulthood as part of in-service training.

Another challenge of using a new language as the language of instruction is the development of teaching materials and appropriate teaching methods. In the case of Basque in the BAC, the materials have to follow the specific regulations of the Spanish Ministry of Education and the Basque Goverment Department of Education. Nowadays teaching materials include not only textbooks but also different types of software and audiovisual materials. Instructional methods in the different models vary depending on whether Basque is used as a medium of instruction or is taught as a school subject. In models B and D, where Basque is used as the language of instruction, the methodological approach is 'content-based' and shares many characteristics with the CLIL (Content and Language Integrated Learning) approach (for further information on CLIL see Marsh, 2007). Basque is also taught as a subject in models B and D and, in these classes, instruction focuses on Basque grammar and discourse and the study of Basque literature. Basque is a school subject in model A and is taught as a second language. The materials used to teach Basque or through the medium of Basque have been specially developed in the Basque Country and are not translated from other languages. The materials used to teach through the medium of Spanish are in many cases the same as those used in Spanish schools outside the BAC or Navarre.

From bilingualism to multilingualism and multiculturalism

So far we have focused on the teaching of Basque as a minority language but the Basque Country has also been affected by the spread of English as a language of wider communication all over the world and the increasing multilingualism and multiculturalism resulting from immigration.

English is not used in everyday life in the BAC but parents feel the need for the new generations to be proficient in English and they demand more instruction in English. One of the characteristics of the educational systems in the BAC and Navarre is the early introduction of English in kindergarten. The idea is that more years of exposure to English will result in higher levels of proficiency. However, research carried out in the Basque Country shows that when exposure to the target language is very limited (2–3 hours per week) younger children do not necessarily make more progress than older children (see García Mayo & Gardía Lecumberri, 2003, Cenoz forthcoming). A further development to increase exposure to English is to use English as an additional language of instruction. Depending on the model, subjects that were originally taught in Basque or in Spanish are taught through the medium of English. There are schools that were originally A or B model schools and now use the three languages as languages or instruction. Some D model schools have introduced English to teach some subjects that were originally taught through Basque. Teaching subjects through English is more demanding for the teacher and also implies the development of specific materials in accordance with the curriculum. The level of proficiency in Basque in models B and D as compared to model A indicates that the use of a language as the medium of instruction is a more efficient way to teach the language than to teach it as a subject even if it is taught from a very early age as it is the case with the A model.

Over the last years, an increasing number of immigrants from Latin America, Africa and some Eastern European countries have been coming to the Basque Country. The most recent figures indicate that the percentage of immigrants in the BAC is 6.5% and 12.2% in Navarre (Instituto Nacional de Estadística, 2008). The Basque Country which was quite homogeneous is becoming more multilingual and multicultural. Some of the immigrant students speak Spanish because they come from Spanish-speaking countries in Latin America but the arrival of speakers of other languages creates a challenge for the school system that already has three languages. It is difficult to predict what the impact of immigration will be on the survival of the Basque language. Most immigrants attend public schools and the percentage of immigrants who have Basque as the language of instruction is much lower than for the total number of students in the BAC (see also Etxeberria & Elosegi, 2008; Cenoz forthcoming). This creates a concentration of immigrant students in some schools, mainly in public schools in the A model. As we have already seen in this article, the results in Basque, Spanish and other areas of the curriculum were already quite low in the A model as compared to other models in the 2004 evaluation when the number of immigrants was not as high. The sample of this 2004 evaluation only included 51 immigrant students (2.4% of the total sample) and almost half of these immigrant students were in the A model in the public network. Nowadays, this concentration still exists but immigrant students are also distributed among the different models and networks.

It is clear that the boundaries between the A, B and D models designed in the early 80's are nowadays blurred because of the increasing number of Spanish-speaking students in the D model, the use of English as an additional language of instruction and the arrival of speakers of other languages. The dynamics of bilingual and multilingual education in the BAC in the last decades has as a result the existence of more types of schools that do not fit into the typology of the three models. These different types are related to: i) the extent to which Basque and English are used as a medium of instruction and ii) the students' home languages. Nowadays, the features of multilingual education in the BAC, Navarre and Iparraldea can better be represented in a model based on continua such as the *'Continua of Multilingual Education'* (see Cenoz forthcoming for a description of the model). This model is a tool to describe different types of multilingual education and highlights the interaction of linguistic, sociolinguistic and educational variables. The basic idea is that different variables in the sociolinguistic context (both at the micro and macro levels) and the educational context can be organized along continua that range from *'less multilingual'* to *'more multilingual'*:

Schools in the BAC have different positions on the continuum "languages of instruction". Some schools have only one language of instruction (Basque or Spanish) and can be placed towards the less multilingual end of the continuum on this variable. Other schools have two languages of instruction: Basque and English, Basque and Spanish, Spanish and English and others three languages of instruction (usually Basque, Spanish and a foreign language which is English in most cases). The more languages of instruction a school has the more multilingual its position is along the continuum. Another factor to be taken into account when defining a school as more or less multilingual refers to the integration of the different languages in syllabus design and language planning so that schools planning together and coordinating the teaching of the different languages of instruction are more multilingual. Other factors are the age in which the different languages are introduced, multilingual proficiency of the teachers or their specific training for multilingual education. The *Continua of Multilingual Education* does not establish hard boundaries between models and can account for the dynamics of bilingual and multilingual education because continua allow for fluidity along the points of the continua (see also Hornberger, 2007).

Future directions

The *Continua of Multilingual Education* is a tool to classify bilingual and multilingual schools from a holistic perspective, taking into account the languages taught at school, the home languages and the sociolinguistic context in which the schools are located. Basque schools have moved from bilingualism to multilingualism in the last years because of the importance of English, the study of French as a fourth language and the arrival of students who speak other languages. In this section a holistic approach will be proposed for research on minority languages.

Adopting a holistic perspective in the study of bilingualism was also proposed by Cook (1995, 2002). According to Cook, bilinguals (and multilinguals) have a unique form of language competence that is not necessarily comparable to that of monolinguals because learning a second or additional language has an influence on the whole cognitive system. Second language users possess unique forms of competence, or competencies, in their own right and should not be seen as the sum of two monolinguals. This perspective has important consequences for the evaluation of proficiency in Basque, Spanish and English in the BAC. Traditionally the reference used in the evaluation of languages has been the educated native speaker of each of the languages. Basque students have been evaluated against the yardstick of an ideal monolingual speaker of Spanish and an ideal monolingual speaker of Basque. According to the evaluations, Basque L1 students who speak Basque at home, use Basque as the language of instruction and live in a Basque-speaking area obtain a very good command of Spanish. However, it may be unrealistic that they achieve exactly the same level of proficiency in Spanish as other students who use Spanish for all purposes all the time except for a very limited number of hours of Basque and English lessons at school (see for example Santiago et al, 2008). Similarly, it cannot be expected that Spanish L1 students who speak Spanish at home and in everyday communication reach the same level of proficiency as Basque speakers even if they have Basque as the main language of instruction (ISEI-IVEI, 2005). If we adopt a holistic view of multilingual proficiency students in the Basque educational system could be evaluated as multilingual speakers who have a linguistic repertoire which is different from that of monolinguals. This linguistic repertoire can also include the home languages of immigrant students and foreign languages such as English or French. A holistic perspective in evaluation and research can also be appropriate to analyse the results of new projects that are integrating the different languages in the curriculum. As Elorza & Muñoa explain (2008: 91) an integrated curriculum '*transfers, applies and generalises what has been learned in one language to the others*'. A holistic view of multilingual proficiency as a reference is more challenging and difficult to put into practice in syllabus design, teaching practice and assessment but it approaches the teaching of different languages from a more realistic approach.

Another point which is related to a holistic approach and which is a real challenge for Basque and other minority languages has to do with the new ways of communication and the effects of new technologies and globalization. Nowadays, the boundaries between languages are soft in daily communication because of the spread use of English and other languages in the media and advertising as it has been seen in studies of the linguistic landscape (Gorter, 2006; Shohamy & Gorter, 2008). At the same time new technologies have blurred the boundaries between oral and written language and have influenced the use of multiple codes combining symbols, images, sounds and printed text. Shohamy (2006: 172) highlights the idea of hybridity in communication resulting from mixing languages and multimodality derived from mixing codes. Students in Basque schools and elsewhere make use of these new types of communication when they interact with their friends and mainly when they use new ways of communication (chats, SMS, etc). From a holistic perspective this is also part of communicative competence and it can be important to conduct research on the use of Basque (and other minority languages) not only in formal settings at school but also in everyday communication between students. The use of Basque in these situations will probably be part of a type of competence where hybridity is salient.

The use of Basque as the main language of instruction in the BAC is well established nowadays. The results of the evaluations show that it is possible to acquire a high level of proficiency in Basque and Spanish by having Basque as the main language of instruction. Teaching through Basque is also compatible with good levels of achievement in other school subjects. However, education in the BAC as elsewhere in the world is a dynamic process and faces new challenges nowadays. In this article we suggest that a more holistic approach to research can be more suitable to understand the increasing diversity of a more multilingual and multicultural world.

Acknowledgements

This article has been written as part of the contribution to the European 6th Framework network of excellence *Sustainable Development in Diverse World* (sus.div). Some of the studies reported in this article have been supported by the Spanish Ministry of Science and Innovation grant *HUM2006-09775-C02-01/FILO and* Basque Government grant IT-202-07.

References

Aldekoa, J. & Gardner, N. 2002. Turning knowledge of Basque into use: Normalization plans for schools. *International Journal for Bilingual Education and Bilingualism* 5: 339–354.
Aiestaran, J. 2003. *Aspects of Language Contact in Rioja Alavesa*. PhD dissertation, Bangor University.
Arzamendi, J. & Genesee, F. 1997. Reflections on immersion education in the Basque Country. In *Immersion Education: International Perspectives*, K. Johnson & M. Swain (eds), 151–166. Cambridge: CUP.
Azurmendi, M.J. & Martínez de Luna, I. 2005. Introduction: Presenting the Basque case. *International Journal of the Sociology of Language* 174: 1–8.
Azurmendi, M.J., Larrañaga, N. & Apalategi, J. 2008. *Bilingualism, Identity and Citizenship in the Basque Country*. In *Bilingualism and Identity*, M. Niño-Murcia & J. Rothman (eds), 35–62. Amsterdam: John Benjamins.

Baetens Beardsmore, H. 1993. The European school model. In *European Models of Bilingual Education*, H. Baetens Beardsmore (ed), 121–154. Clevedon: Multilingual Matters.

Basque Government. 2008. *IV Inkesta Soziolinguistikoa* Vitoria-Gasteiz: Basque Government.

Carder, M. 2007. *Bilingualism in International Schools*. Clevedon: Mulltilingual Matters.

Cenoz, J. 2002. Three languages in contact: Language attitudes in the Basque Country. In *Language Awareness in the Foreign Language Classroom*, D. Lasagabaster & J. Sierra (eds.), 37–60. Leioa: Universidad del País Vasco.

Cenoz, J. 1992. *Enseñanza-aprendizaje del inglés como L2 o L3*. Bilbao: University of the Basque Country.

Cenoz, J. 2003. The additive effect of bilingualism on third language acquisition: A review. *The International Journal of Bilingualism* 7: 71–88.

Cenoz, J. 2008a. The status of Basque in the Basque Country. In *Mapping Linguistic Diversity in Multicultural Contexts*, M. Barni & G. Extra (eds.), 93–113. Berlin: Mouton de Gruyter.

Cenoz, J. (ed.). 2008b. Teaching through Basque: Achievements and challenges. Special issue of *Language Culture and Curriculum* 21(1).

Cenoz, J. 2005. English in bilingual programs in the Basque Country. *International Journal of the Sociology of Language* 171: 41–56.

Cenoz, J. Forthcoming. *Towards Multilingual Education: Basque Educational Research in International Perspective*. Clevedon: Multilingual Matters.

Cenoz, J. & Valencia, J. 1994. Additive trilingualism: Evidence from the Basque Country. *Applied Psycholinguistics* 15: 157–209.

Cook, V. 1995. Multi-competence and the learning of many languages. *Language, Culture and Curriculum* 8: 93–98.

Cook, V. 2002. Background to the L2 user. In *Portraits of the L2 User*, V. Cook (ed.), 1–28. Clevedon: Multilingual Matters.

Council of Europe 1992. *European Charter for Regional or Minority Languages*. Strasbourg: Council of Europe.

De Mejia, A.M. 2002. *Power, Prestige and Bilingualism*. Clevedon: Multilingual Matters.

Elorza, I. & I. Muñoa. 2008. Promoting the minority language through integrated plurilingual language planning: The case of the ikastolas. *Language, Culture and Curriculum* 21: 85–101.

Etxeberria, F. & Elosegi, K. 2008. Basque, Spanish and immigrant minority languages in the Basque School. *Language Culture and Curriculum* 21: 69–84.

García Mayo, M.P. & García Lecumberri, M.L. (eds). 2003. *Age and the Acquisition of English as a Foreign Language: Theoretical Issues and Field Work*. Clevedon: Multilingual Matters.

Genesee, F. 1987. *Learning Through Two Languages: Studies of Immersion and Bilingual Education*. Cambridge MA: Newbury House.

Gorter, D. 2006. Linguistic landscape: A new approach to multilingualism. Special issue of *International Journal of Multilingualism* 3.

Hamel, R. 2007. Bilingual education for indigenous communities in Mexico. In *Encyclopedia of Language and Education*, Vol 5, *Bilingual Education*, J. Cummins & N. Hornberger (eds), 311–322. New York NY: Springer.

Hornberger, N. (2007) Continua of biliteracy. In *Encyclopedia of Language and Education*, Vol 9, *Ecology of Language*, A. Creese, P. Martin & N. Hornberger (eds), 275–290. Berlin: Springer.

Instituto Nacional de Estadística, 2008. *Demografía y Población*. http://www.ine.es

ISEI-IVEI. 2005. Level B2 in Basque at the end of obligatory education http://www.isei-ivei.net/eng/pubeng/B2_ENGLISH1.pdf.

ISEI-IVEI. 2006. ISEI-IVEI (2006b) Evaluación de la educación primaria 2004. http://www.isei-ivei.net/cast/pub/indexpub.htm.

ISEI-IVEI. 2008. Informe final de la Evaluación PISA 2006. http://www.isei-ivei.net/cast/pub/indexpub.htm.

Lasagabaster, D. 1998. *Creatividad y conciencia metalingüística: Incidencia en el aprendizaje del inglés como L3.* Bilbao: University of the Basque Country.

López, L.E. & Sichra, I. 2007. Intercultural bilingual education among indigenous peoples in Latin America. In *Encyclopedia of Language and Education*, Vol 5, *Bilingual Education*, J. Cummins & N. Hornberger (eds), 295–309. Berlin: Springer.

Marsh, C. 2007. Language awareness and CLIL In *Encyclopedia of Language and Education*, Vol 6, *Knowledge about Language*, J. Cenoz & N. Hornberger (eds), 233–246. Berlin: Springer,

McCarty, T.L., Romero, M.E. & O. Zepeda. 2006. Reimagining multilingual America: Lessons from native American youth. In *Imagining Multilingual Schools*, O. García, T. Skutnabb-Kangas & M.E. Guzmán (eds), 91–110. Clevedon: Multilingual Matters.

Oroz, N. & Sotés, P. 2008. Bilingual education in Navarre. *Language, Culture and Curriculum* 21: 21–38.

Sagasta, M.P. 2003. Acquiring writing skills in a third language: The positive effects of bilingualism. *International Journal of Bilingualism* 7: 27–42

Santiago, K., Lukas, J.F., Moyano, N., Lizasoain, L. & Joaristi, L. 2008. A longitudinal study of academic achievement in Spanish: The effect of linguistic models. *Language, Culture and Curriculum* 2: 48–58.

Shohamy, E. 2006. Imagined multilingual schools: How come we don't deliver? In *Imagining Multilingual Schools*, O. García, T. Skutnabb-Kangas & M.E. Guzmán (eds), 171–183. Clevedon: Multilingual Matters.

Shohamy, E. & Gorter, D. (eds). 2009. *Linguistic Landscape: Expanding the Scenery.* London: Routledge.

Zalbide, M. & Cenoz, J. 2008. Bilingual education in the Basque Autonomous Community: Achievements and challenges. *Language, Culture and Curriculum* 21: 5–20.

Author's address

Jasone Cenoz
Department of Research Methods in Education, FICE
University of the Basque Country
Tolosa Hiribidea 70
20018 San Sebastian, Spain

jasone.cenoz@ehu.es

Language-in-education policies
in the Catalan language area

F. Xavier Vila i Moreno
University of Barcelona

The territories where Catalan is traditionally spoken as a native language constitute an attractive sociolinguistic laboratory which appears especially interesting
from the point of view of language-in-education policies. The educational system
has spearheaded the recovery of Catalan during the last 20 years. Schools are
being attributed most of the responsibility for the (failure of integration) of past
and current immigrant waves.

There is a historical, demolinguistic and political fragmentation of the
linguistic area of Catalan because at least 8 different national and sub-national
authorities have a say in the definition of language policies in education. This cir-
cumstance has led to the establishment of a number of school models which deal
differently with each of the challenges described before. In this contribution, an
overview is produced of the main school models which are currently running in
the Catalan language areas from a comparative perspective, highlighting their
points in common and their differences. The article also provides a summary of
available research results in connection with language learning, language practices, the impact on social integration and cohesion, and on academic achievement. It does review some of the challenges that will have to be faced by each
system in the near future.

The Catalan language area: Some historical facts

Catalan is a Romance language, i.e., an Indo-European language closely related to Oc-
citan, French, Italian and Spanish. It is the autochthonous language of a geographical
area divided over four states, namely Spain, France, Andorra and Italy. In Spain, the
historical Catalan language area covers Catalonia; most of Valencia (also called the
Valencian Country or Valencian Community); the Balearic Islands; a stretch of land in
Aragon on the border with Catalonia, known as La Franja; and a handful of hamlets
in Murcia Region known as *Carxe/Carche*. In France, Catalan is the historical language of the Department of Eastern Pyrenees (*Catalunya Nord*, 'Northern Catalonia'

AILA Review 21 (2008), 31–48. DOI 10.1075/aila.21.04vila
ISSN 1461–0213 / E-ISSN 1570–5595 © John Benjamins Publishing Company

in Catalan), also known as *Rosselló/Roussillon*. Catalan is the historical and sole official language of Andorra, the small independent state in the Pyrenees. Finally, Catalan is also the traditional language of the Sardinian city of Alghero (*l'Alguer* in Catalan), in Italy, since the 14th century.

In historical terms, Catalan derives from the Latin imported two thousand years ago to what is now Catalonia, Andorra and Northern Catalonia by Roman settlers. A short introduction into the social history of Catalan is provided by Hall (2001), De Melchior, Vicent and Branchadell (2002) or Ferrando and Nicolás (1993). In the thirteenth century, Catalan spread to Valencia and the Balearic Islands after their being conquered and annexed to the dual Crown formed by Catalonia and Aragon. The language became standardized and flourished between the 13th and 15th centuries. As the language of power in the Crown of Aragon, it was used for clerical, literary, scientific, philosophical and, of course, practical purposes such as medicine or gastronomy treaties.

The position of Catalan weakened abruptly by the turning from the 15th to the 16th centuries. In less than half a century, Catalan passed from being the language of the Crown of Aragon, a Mediterranean economic and military power, to find itself in a peripheral position within the Habsburg's multinational empire. Soon, the imperial authorities became associated with the kingdom of Castile and with Castilian, a country that was beginning its Golden Century. Thus, within a few decades, the Catalan culture lost its vibrancy, and Catalonian, Valencian and Balearic cultural elites contented themselves with consuming imported Castilian culture. The *Decadència* ('Decay') of Catalan literature and cultural life had started.

Castilian — also known as *Spanish* — is the historical denomination of the language born and developed in the Kingdom of Castile, which eventually spread to the rest of the Hispanic Empire, much in the same way as English, the language of England, spread across the British Empire. In fact, the term *castellano* is very widely used both among L1 and L2 speakers, to the extent that the current Spanish Constitution (art. 3) says: «Castilian is the official Spanish language of the State (…) The other Spanish languages shall also be official in their respective Autonomous Communities…». In the Spanish context, the use of *español* ('*Spanish*') to refer to *Castilian* has more often than not been associated with non-pluralistic, non-egalitarian positions which try to grant Castilian a hegemonic role all over Spain as *the* language of Spain.

In 1659, and as a result of the Treaty of the Pyrenees, the Catalan counties of Roussillon and Cerdagne were annexed by France and became subject to France's language policies. The institutional position of Castilian in the Catalan language area was greatly reinforced after the Spanish War of Succession (1700–1714). The new king Philip V issued the *Nueva Planta* decrees, which put an end to the wide autonomy of the kingdoms of the Crown of Aragon. Since then, the successive administrations showed increasing zeal in pursuing the linguistic homogenisation of Spain by spreading the knowledge and use of Castilian. The administration, the army, part of the Catholic church, the incipient cultural industries and mass media, and, of course, education became agents to promote language shift (see Ferrer 1985). The military dictatorships of Miguel Primo de Rivera (1923–1929) and especially Francisco Franco (1936/39–1975) were particularly severe in their anticatalan practices, but assimilationist goals and policies were not restricted to dictatorial periods; in fact, even in the most liberal parliamentary regimes such as the II Spanish Republic (1931–1936/39) efforts were made by the central power to grant and preserve a hegemonic place for Castilian in the Catalan-speaking area (see Vila 2008).

Language-in-education policy is one, if not *the* one field, where language policies have changed most during the last decades. Between the 18th to 20th centuries, the educational system had been a key agency to promote language shift from Catalan to the official languages (Pueyo 1996). Thus, schools to teach French language and culture were established in Northern Catalonia already in the late 17th century, a short time after the annexation (cf. Ferrer 1985: 25). In the south, the Spanish King Charles III imposed that primary education should be in Castilian already in 1768 (Real Cédual de Aranjuez). Once education was declared universal and compulsory by mid-19th century, the school's capacity to promote the State language increased exponentially (Pueyo 1996).

In this context, the Catalan-speaking population started to learn the State language and to internalise its hegemonic position vis-à-vis Catalan. Both processes were speeded up by the massive immigration of native speakers of the official languages during the 20th century, and by the always increasing presence of mass media. Thus, between 1900 and 1950 monolingual Catalan speakers gradually disappeared, replaced by bilinguals and, in some areas, monolingual speakers of the official languages.

By the 1970's, in many respects, it could be said that policies leading to the extinction of Catalan had almost succeeded. The nation-state languages had become prevalent in the Catalan language areas as never before in history, not only in legal, but also in socio-demographic terms. The trends leading towards total language shift were so well established that the disappearance of Catalan appeared to be just a matter of a (very) few generations. But things evolved in a different direction.

The last decades of the 20th and early 21st centuries witnessed a remarkable change in language policies regarding Catalan. On the one hand, the nation-state structures changed. In Spain, changes were deeply connected with the evolution from Franco's dictatorship to a constitutional, parliamentary monarchy with a semi-federal structure known as the 'State of autonomies', which allowed national minorities to make their voices heard, at least to a certain extent, and even implement partly autonomous language policies. As a consequence, the three largest Catalan-speaking societies — i.e., Catalonia, Valencia and Balearic Islands — started to develop their own language-in-education policies.

Simultaneously, the general ideological context was evolving. A new political culture — new discourses, new ideologies, new practices — slowly emerged that was more respectful with the individuals' linguistic preferences and with linguistic diversity in general (Spolsky 2004). Ironically — or not so —, once the state language was effectively becoming socially hegemonic, the state's legitimacy to impose one given language was eroded. This new discourses had an impact all over the Catalan-speaking area, and opened new spaces for Catalan in the educational system also in France and Italy.

Contemporary language-in-education policies and models

Language-in-education policies and models in Spain

Contemporary language policies in Spain have become much more pluralistic than they used to be until 1978. Of course, Castilian remains the State's sole official language, but Catalan has become official also in almost all its historical territories, namely Catalonia, Valencia and Balearic Islands. All school children — i.e., including non-Catalan L1 — living in these territories must learn both official languages..

The key to understanding this new arrangement lies on the distribution of power: since the late 70's, language policy has been distributed among the central and the autonomous authorities, and each autonomous government has developed its own language policy, also in the field of education. These models, though, are not independent. In the education field, the 1978 Constitution (Arts. 149.1.30 and 27) reserves for the central authorities the "basic elements of the curriculum". The current Education Bill makes these elements equivalent to 55% of class hours in those autonomous communities with their own language other than Castilian. In other words, the governments of the autonomous communities have a considerable amount of room for manoeuvre, when it comes to establishing the language models to be followed in schools. But an overview of these models shows that they may be substantially different from each other.

School language models in Catalonia

The definition and implementation of the school model in Catalonia was initially based on Article 14 of Catalonia's 1983 Linguistic Normalisation Act. In 1994, a ruling of Spain's Constitutional Court declared that the *model de conjunció en català* ('conjunction in Catalan model') was constitutional, which sped up its implementation (Constitutional Court Ruling 337/1994, of 23 December). Essentially, the conjunction model makes Catalan the normal medium of instruction. Catalan and Castilian must have a proper presence in curricula so that their normal and correct use by all students is assured by the end of compulsory education. Initial instruction in Castilian is in theory granted to parents who apply for it, although this only happens on very rare occasions. At the same time, schools with large percentages of non-Catalan speakers may take advantage of language immersion programmes and other programmes.

The education system in Catalonia has progressively been adopting Catalan as its language of teaching, especially in primary education: official figures (see Table 1) place teaching in Catalan at above 90% of primary schools and at practically 50% in

Table 1. Students in public and private schools by language in which classes are taught. Catalonia. Infant and primary, secondary education (1999–2000)

Language in which classes are taught	Primary	Secondary
In Catalan	92	49
Predominantly in Catalan	2	36
In Catalan and Castilian	2	15
No information	4	
Total	100	100

Source: School census drawn up by the Catalan Teaching Service of the Department of Education of the *Generalitat de Catalunya*

secondary schools. Taking into account that the law states that Catalan must be used as the language of instruction, these figures may be higher than the actual practice in the schools but in any case, they show the best-ever situation in terms of the presence of Catalan in the country's classrooms.

The Language Policy Act of 1998 consolidated this model in Catalonia. In 2006 Catalonia approved by referendum a new Statute of Autonomy which includes (Art. 35) the essential elements of this linguistic model, including the right of newly-arrived students to receive special help with the language.

Although in general terms the school model in Catalonia seems quite well established, a number of issues remain somehow open and may lead to changes in the future. In spite of the model being declared constitutional in the 1994, animosity against it in Castilian-speaking Spain remains quite widespread and vociferous, and attempts to modify it using the central institutions are not rare. For instance, in 2007 the Spanish government required schools to teach an extra hour of Castilian language, a point which became quite controversial in Catalonia and created strong tensions within the government. Opposition to the model is much weaker in Catalonia: *Ciudadanos*, a party promoted by Castilian-language activists reached 3% and 3 seats in the Catalan parliament in 2006 elections. A more relevant issue are the debates surrounding the overall quality of education. Schools in Catalonia seem to be promoting equity, but not excellence and a Bill of Education is currently under debate and will be soon presented to the Parliament.

School language models in the Balearic Islands

The definition of the school language model in the Balearic Islands occurred much more recently than in Catalonia, and it is more closely linked to the political situation. According to Article 20.1 of the Islands' Language Normalisation Act of 1986 schoolchildren should be able to use Catalan and Castilian correctly at the end of their compulsory education. However, the conservative government of the Balearic Islands did not pass the so-called "Decree of Minimums", requiring that at least half of the subjects be taught in Catalan until 1997 (Decree 92/1997, of 4 July, confirmed by a

Table 2. Language of teaching in infant and primary schools. Balearic Islands (2002–03)

Language of teaching	Number of centres	%
Catalan	181	57
More Catalan than Castilian	84	26
Compulsory minimum in Catalan (50%)	55	17
Total	320	100

Source: Dept. of Education and Culture, Government of the Balearic Islands

ruling of the Spanish Supreme Court of 4 October 2002). It was not until the next centre-leftist "Pact of Progress" government (1999–2003) that the measures to ensure effective compliance with this decree were implemented, including a provision that all teachers should demonstrate knowledge of Catalan (cf. Pons and Vila 2005: 141–143). By the 2002–2003 academic year, a majority of primary schools declared to be using Catalan as their main medium of instruction (see Table 2). As far as secondary education was concerned, Catalan was used to teach between 60 and 80% of subjects.

In 2003, the conservatives returned to government in the Balearic Islands and passed a decree designed in principle to encourage the use of foreign languages in teaching, but allowing for a reduction in the use of Catalan to only one third of the teaching hours. This is the Trilingualism or *Fiol* Decree (Decree 52/2006, of 16 June, BOIB of 20-06-2006). These and other initiatives encountered strong opposition from the education community and very few centres took their provisions on board. The new centre-leftist government elected as a result of the 2007 elections stopped the pressure to reduce the use of Catalan as medium of instruction, announced measures to spread trilingual education, and integration of foreign immigrants arrived during the 2000's.

School language models in Valencia

Historically Valencia is divided into two linguistic areas where Castilian is spoken in the inner-most areas and Valencian is spoken on the coast. Valencian is the name most commonly used in the Autonomous Community of Valencia when referring to Catalan. The Community of Valencia has experienced a deeper process of language shift towards Castilian and the Valencian language-in-education policy has followed a path which is quite different from those in Catalonia and the Balearic Islands. In practice, bilingual education is only available in the Catalan-speaking areas, and the school system is organized along linguistic lines or programmes (Decree 79/1984, of 30 July, on non-university education):

1. The *Progressive Incorporation [into Valencian] Programme* (PIP), in which Castilian is the language of teaching and Valencian is a compulsory subject and that of teaching in some areas of knowledge;

2. The *Teaching in Valencian Programme* (PEV), in which Valencian is the language of teaching and Castilian is a compulsory subject and the language in which some areas of knowledge are taught;
3. The *Linguistic Immersion in Valencian Programme* (PIL), aimed at students whose first language is not Valencian and in which teaching is carried out in Valencian, with Castilian being introduced progressively from the third year of primary school as a language of teaching.

In secondary education, only the first two models (i.e. the PIP and the PEV) are applied. For their part, in the Castilian-speaking areas, there is only one school language mode, called the *Basic Programme*, in which the language of teaching is Castilian and the teaching of Valencian is declared compulsory. In practice, however, the teaching of Catalan in this area has become optional and is carried out only if the school community is interested.

Assessing the importance of the PEV and the PIL in the overall Valencian education system is a difficult task but Baldaquí (personal communication), calculates that teaching in Valencian (i.e. following the PEV and/or PIL) only covers 24.2% of students in Valencia (Table 3). These figures show a sharp drop from primary to secondary education, due to the lack of availability in both the public and private sectors rather than to any lack of demand. Furthermore, teaching in Valencian is much more common in public than in private schools.

Early education in foreign languages has been introduced by means of the Enriched Bilingual Education Programme (PEBE),[1] which is combined with one of the existing ones (PIL, PEV or PIP). This programme can also be applied in Castilian-speaking districts. This means that, in addition to teaching in a foreign language, the school must carry out a minimum amount of teaching in Catalan. This is the Enriched Basic Programme (PBE, in its Castilian/Catalan initials). The 1998–99 academic year saw 53 schools implementing it, a figure which had risen to 278 by that of 2006–07. It is worth noting that, in this latter year, the majority of schools applying the PEBE (160) were public centres included in the programmes in Valencian (PEV/PIL) (source: http://www.cult.gva.es/sedev/).

Table 3. Students in Valencia according to means of instruction. Year 2006–07.

	Infant (2nd cycle) and Primary education	Secondary education	TOTAL
PIL or PEV (Catalan medium)	122,241 (28.7%)	47,612 (17.3%)	169,853 (24.2%)
Basic programme (Castilian medium)	303,527 (71.3%)	228,265 (82.7%)	531,792 (75.8%)
Total	425,768 (100%)	275,877 (100%)	701,645 (100%)

Source: Josep Maria Baldaquí, (personal communication). University of Alacant

School language models in la Franja (Aragon)

Catalan in *la Franja* is not an official language. Aragon's reformed Statute of 2007 does not give the language any official status and leaves to a future law provisions on its use in education (Art. 7.2). As a consequence, the language presence in school is very weak. In 1985, within the framework of the collaboration agreement with Spain's Ministry of Education and Science,[2] schools in *la Franja* began to teach Catalan on a voluntary and optional basis. The agreement allows for a progressive expansion of Catalan teaching, with the result that, today, almost all primary school students and half of the secondary ones take Catalan classes. Catalan classes began in the 1984–85 academic year with 700 students but this number increased to 3,496 by 2004–05 (see Table 4). Additionally, a number of secondary schools have some experience of teaching partially through the medium of Catalan.

Table 4. Catalan language teaching in *la Franja*. 2004–05

Level	Taking Catalan	% of total	Total
Primary	2,612	87	3,007
Secondary	884	68	1,297
Total	3,496	81	4,304

Source: Aragon's Dept. of Education

Although most students in this area take Catalan classes there are only between two and four hours of Catalan per week. Bearing in mind that Catalan is not an official language and has little written or formal presence, these few hours of teaching do not even guarantee that native Catalan speakers will be able to properly read or write their own language. Non-native pupils do not acquire productive competence with these classes either.

The language-in-education models in Andorra

Andorra is a small state in the Pyrenees which has managed to remain independent from either Spain and France, and Catalan is its only official language. Once a rural, poor country, Andorra became a pole of tourist and financial attraction during the second half of the 20th century. In 1940, 17% of Andorra's population already consisted of *foreigners* — basically Catalonians (Planelles 1999: 233). But in the following decades, the ethnolinguistic landscape of Andorra changed dramatically, with the arrival of Castilian-speaking Spaniards, French, Portuguese, and eventually people from a wide variety of origins. Thus, in 2004 only 28,2% of Andorrans older than 14 years had an Andorran passport (Torres et al 2006: 16).

The educational landscape in Andorra is quite complex and several educational systems coexist on its territory: the Andorran system, the French system, and the Spanish system. The reason for this complexity goes back in history: during a good part of the 20th century, Andorrans were content to be served basically by foreign educational systems — the French and the Spanish — which granted them free education and access to universities. Massive immigration of non-Catalan speakers in the 60's and 70's changed the *status quo*, and Andorra changed its educational policy to develop a national educational system. On the one hand, the authorities required the teaching of Catalan and Andorran history and culture in all systems. On the other, a new Andorran educational system was created. This new system focussed from the inception on bilingual schools, with Catalan as the main language of instruction and an important role attributed to French. This design was rooted in Andorra's sociolinguistic situation: for decades, most Andorrans — with Catalan as their L1 — used to attend the French system to acquire French, while Castilian was much easier to pick up due to the large amount of Castilian residents in the country. And the design proved to be wise: today, the Andorran system has become the predominant in terms of the public served: thus, in September 2008, 4.065 pupils were attending the Andorran system, compared to 3.680 in the French one and 3.452 in the Spanish one (Source: Diari d'Andorra, September 10th, http://www.diariandorra.ad/noticies/view.php?ID=8408).

The language-in-education models in Northern Catalonia (France) and l'Alguer/Alghero (Italy)[3]

Official language policies, demographic movements and massive language shift have put Catalan in Northern Catalonia and in l'Alguer/Alghero in a very delicate position (cf. Querol *et al.* 2007). In both territories, intergenerational language transmission within the families has been massively interrupted during the 20th century; therefore, the educational system has become the most important social institution where Catalan can be acquired. The position of Catalan in the educational systems of both territories has improved during the last decades; nevertheless, it remains peripheral and fragile.

Like the rest of regional and minority languages in France, mainstream schools in Northern Catalonian work in French and Catalan courses in schools are optional. Although they are on the increase, only a minority of pupils receive any effective teaching of Catalan at all. The teaching of Catalan may proceed along three different paths. In the first case, Catalan lessons are offered in quite a number of mainstream schools. A second option of Catalan language learning is provided by 12 *bilingual* schools, which serve around 1.350 pupils. The linguistic model of these schools is quite heterogeneous, and spans from very weak use of Catalan to equal amounts of use of French and Catalan. These schools aim at bilingualism in terms of language competence and attitudes, but do not work actively to encourage the reintroduction of Catalan in interpersonal communication.

Finally, there exists a private, partly subsidised network of Catalan-medium schools called La Bressola, i.e. 'the cradle' (La Bressola 2007).[4] In 2006–07 this network served more than 600 children up from pre-school (2 years old) to secondary education in 8 centres. La Bressola schools use Catalan as their main language of instruction and encourage the interpersonal use of Catalan among children while preserving the highest levels of French and making significant efforts to teach English. In general, demand for Catalan is well over offer (Becat 2000), especially in the case of the La Bressola network.

The social situation of Catalan in the Sardinian city of l'Alguer/Alghero is fragile, with an almost total interruption of intergenerational transmission (Chessa 2007). Nevertheless, a number of initiatives have been launched in order to reverse the process. In the school arena, two major initiatives deserve being mentioned. On the one hand, since 1998, the Palomba Project has taught Alguerese Catalan to primary education children of almost all local schools. On the other hand, a trilingual (Catalan/Italian/English) school 'La Costura' opened in 2004–05. This school enjoys the support of the local City Council as well as of Catalonia's Department of Education. In several aspects, this schools is based upon the experience of La Bressola where Catalan is the main language of instruction and interpersonal use of this language is encouraged.

Increasing complexity: 'new immigrations' and new languages

Until quite recently, immigration to the Catalan-speaking area used to arrive from neighbouring territories and speak either Catalan or the state's official language. In the late 90's and early 2000's, the migratory processes increased again, but this time immigrants arrived from many other countries. In 10 years, percentages of foreigners in the Catalan language area passed from less than 2% to 15% and more (Pons and Vila 2005).

These *new immigrants*, as they are often called to distinguish them from older immigrants coming from the same nation-state — have substantially modified both the teaching reality and the public discourses about language-in-education practices in the Catalan language area. In general terms, adult and young new immigrants have tended to use Castilian (French or Italian) to interact with locals, whether this was the immigrants' first language (as in the case most Latin-Americans) or not. This process has pushed Catalan a little bit more to a peripheral position, especially in Northern Catalonia and several areas of Valencia. Immigrant children tend to concentrate in the public schools. In Catalonia, for instance, public schools serve 85% of foreign pupils, while subsidised private schools[5] serve only 15% of these pupils. Many public schools have to deal with a disproportionately high percentage of newly arrived children, and these tend to have lower educational standards and/or little mastery of the school language(s). According to Pisa 2006 results in Catalonia, foreign-born pupils scored 71 points below natives in sciences, 66 point in maths, and 72 points in reading comprehension (Ferrer, Valiente and Castel 2008: 8). The pupils' misdistribution sets off the well-known vicious circle which starts with local students leaving for other schools and leaving behind empty places to be filled by other newly arrived pupils. This process can lead to *ghetto schools* where locals are a minority as compared to immigrant students (for Catalonia, see Síndic 2008). The concentration of foreign pupils in some tracts of the educational system increases the problems of social segregation and inequity (Ferrer, 2008).

The reaction towards this sudden immigration has taken a number of forms. To speak only about Catalonia, specific treatment for foreign students started with the School adaptation workshops (*tallers d'adaptació escolars*), which offered linguistic support for non-Catalan-speaking children (Purtí 2006). Once the new administration was set up in November 2003, a Plan for the Language and Social Cohesion (*Pla per la llengua i la cohesió social*)[6] was launched, which made a strong emphasis on connecting the learning of Catalan with the social and scholar integration of newcomer children. Central to the plan were the *welcoming classes* programme (*aules d'acollida*), whereby newly arrived children were integrated in mainstream classes since the first day, and pulled out for some hours of Catalan language learning. Other initiatives have been those of *Educational Surrounding Plans* (*Plans Educatius d'Entorn*), whereby schools build a network of cooperation with other educational agents such as local authorities, local cultural or social organisations, in an attempt to involve the whole community in the learning process. Most recently *Educatorial Welcoming Spaces* (*Espais de benvinguda educative*) were created in a number of cities as places where foreign children can receive some primary notions of Catalan and school life before being integrated in mainstream classes.

An overview of the results

Although a considerable amount of work has been done, the dramatic changes that have taken place during the last decades in the Catalan language area in the area of language(-in-education) policies have not been sufficiently analysed in terms of results. Nevertheless, some conclusions on a number of issues can be extracted.

Impact on language competence

In general terms, the introduction of Catalan as a subject and, *a fortiori*, as a language of instruction has had the expected outcome of raising, even if modestly, the competence in this language among the pupils involved. But the actual nature of this increase in competence depends on a number of factors.

In those territories and/or systems where Catalan is the main means of instruction, non-native speakers become proficient in this language. Thus, in Catalonia, where Catalan has become the main language of instruction, the capacity to use this language is becoming universal among the new generations. According to the last official survey (2003) among 15–29 years old, 95% can speak Catalan and 94% can write it; these figures are higher than the 85% and 62% for the population above 14 as a whole (Vila 2005: 33). At the same time, competence in Castilian remains high and quite similar to the general standards in Spain (see Arnau 2004 for a review). Indeed, surveys indicate that secondary education students evaluate their competence in Castilian as higher than in Catalan (Consell Superior d'Avaluació 2008).

On the contrary, in those territories or systems where Catalan is only a school subject, non-native speakers do not become productively bilingual. In Valencia, for instance, 58% of the population aged 15–24 reports to speak Catalan "perfectly" or "quite well", a figure which is quite similar to the 53% of the general population (Acadèmia Valenciana de la Llengua 2005: 39 and 40). Thus, a weak presence of the weak language in the educational system is not enough to turn majority speakers into bilinguals. In Valencia, the most positive results are those of Catalan native speakers taught through the medium of Catalan because they become literate in their first language: 58% of youngsters can write Catalan "perfectly" or "quite well", in comparison to 25% for the whole population (*ibid*, 49 and 50).

Impact on the language system

In general terms, Catalan is quite a homogeneous language, and all varieties are mutually comprehensible. The standard variety allows for a considerable degree of regional variation, linguistic ideologies in the area are in general quite favourable to preserving dialectal diversity, and both linguistic and educational authorities insist on the need to respect the (children's) local varieties (Areny 2002). Nevertheless, contact with written and non-local varieties appears to be promoting changes in the varieties spoken by the new generations, and the school seems to be a key actor in this process, both as an active provider of linguistic models and as an institution for social contact. In very general terms, a process of levelling and/or standardization seems to be in process, with more local features receding in front of regional or more general features. But neither the origin nor the direction of these processes is easy to predict. While many voices alert against a process of linguistic levelling (see Alturo and Vila (eds.), 2002), in some areas, such as the ones in Western Catalonia studied by Carrera (2002), children's phonology is closer to spelling and different from the most widely used spoken standard.

In fact, the school's specific impact on language change may be easier to assess in areas where Catalan is weaker rather than in those areas where its effect is combined with that of the media and the administration. In the southernmost area of Alacant (Alicante), for instance, where Catalan is socially much weaker than in Catalonia, Baldaquí (2006) has measured intergenerational language change in terms of lexicon, morphology and phonetics, and has compared results for children attending Catalan-medium schools and those attending Castilian-medium schools. In general terms, it is difficult for schools to counteract the pressure of the dominant language in areas such as phonetics and morphology but proves to be more effective in the case of the lexicon. Indeed, Catalan-medium schools manage to reduce the frequency of *undue* loanwords from Castilian.

Impact on language use

One of the most complex challenges faced by the educational systems all over the Catalan language area is that of encouraging the interpersonal use of Catalan. Since the second half of the 20th century, virtually all Catalan native speakers have become quite proficient in the state language. At the same time, they have also internalized a linguistic etiquette which makes them switch to the nation-state official language when addressing an out-group member. This strategy is known as *the subordination or automatic convergence language norm*. The obvious outcome of such sociolinguistic norm is that non-Catalan speakers in Catalan speaking territories do not feel the need to learn Catalan.

As the most powerful language policy institution supporting Catalan, schools are expected to modify this situation. In the 70's and 80's, it was commonly assumed that by teaching Catalan *the subordination norm* would disappear and Catalan L2 speakers would start using Catalan. It soon became obvious that in spite of receiving Catalan language lessons, Castilian L1 children were not using Catalan (cf. Bastardas 1985, 1986; Boix 1990). In fact, even where Catalan became the predominant language of education, *the subordination norm* proved very resistant. In his research on language choice and code-switching in a predominantly Castilian-speaking city in the area of Barcelona, Vila (1996) showed that Catalan children continued to address their class-mates in Castilian in classes where Catalan was used as the medium of instruction. In fact, Castilian L1 children only switched to Catalan to address their teachers, and not even in all cases. Further research in other sociolinguistic contexts confirms these findings (Unamuno 1997, or Rosselló 2003; for a state of the art in Catalonia, see Galindo and Vila 2008: 39–57). Thus, the project on language use in the 6th grade of primary education all over Catalonia (see Vila, Vial and Galindo 2005; Galindo 2006; Galindo and Vila 2008) proved that at least in Catalonia there was a direct link between the proportion of Catalan L1 children within a given school and the use of this language. The transcriptions of spontaneous conversations on the playground proved that Castilian-speakers use Catalan actively only in schools where Catalan-speakers are a clear majority.

Why is this so? The Catalan experience shows clearly that linguistic routines, i.e., sociolinguistic norms or etiquette, tend to reproduce between generations in spite of school action. Monitored school interaction accounts for just a small amount of children's significant interaction. Schools alone cannot be expected to modify the norms of behaviour. In most cases, it is the very Catalan L1 parents who unconsciously teach their children to switch when addressing a non-Catalan speaker. Non-Catalan L1 children learn in everyday interaction that it is common for the other speakers to switch to Spanish.

However, the influence of the schools to counteract the pressure of the dominant language also exists. Research by Gomàriz (in press) suggests that the adoption of Catalan as the main means of instruction encourages the use of Catalan as the school *lingua franca* when substantial percentages of speakers of other languages — in this case, Amazigh-speakers — are in contact with a large number of Catalan speakers. La Bressola experience appears as quite remarkable. Although consistent research is not yet available, all information suggests that its immersion system does manage to reintroduce Catalan as the language of interpersonal communication (cf. La Bressola 2007). Another example of the increasing use of Catalan comes from the Balearic Islands where the percentage of university entrance tests taken in Catalan has increased as a consequence of the enhanced position of this language at school: 65,8% in June 2004, 70,9% in June 2005, and 72,4% in June 2006 (Pons and Sorolla in press). In other words, introducing the language into the schools has an impact on language practices, although it should not be overestimated.

Impact on non-linguistic academic results

The results of the educational systems all over Spain are right now under severe scrutiny, especially after the poor results from the successive PISA reports. The Highest Council for the Evaluation of the Educational System of Catalonia offered a balance of accomplishment of the five European educational goals set as a consequence of the Lisbon European Council (March 2000) (CSASE 2007: 121–137). According to these goals:

1. According to 2006 Pisa Report, 21.2% of Catalonia's pupils only attained level 1 or lower in reading comprehension abilities; just a little bit above the OCDE (20.1%), but still lower than the Spanish mean (25.7%).
2. In 2006, 28.6% of Catalonia's population between 18 and 24 with compulsory secondary education did not continue their studies; this figure is sensibly above the 15.1% mean for the European Union (25 member-states), but very similar to the Spanish mean (29.9%).
3. In 2006, Catalonia was also lagging behind the 25 members UE in terms of population successfully finishing post obligatory secondary education: only 65.7% between 20 and 24 years in Catalonia, compared to 77.7% UE-25. But Catalonia's figures remained higher than those of Spain (61.6%).
4. Catalonia was doing relatively well in the number of people between 20 and 29 with a degree in maths, sciences and technology per 1,000 inhabitants: 17.2 in Catalonia, compared to 13.2 in UE-25 and 11.8 in Spain as a whole.
5. In 2006, the percentage of adult population (25–64 years) taking part in formation courses was very similar in Catalonia (9.7%), Spain (10.5%) and EU-25 (10.1%).

In a more critical perspective, Ferrer et al's (2008) study of 2006 Pisa results points out that Catalonia's educational system (a) finds itself on the European mean in terms of equity; (b) well under the European mean in terms of excellence — i.e., excellent students are scarcer in numbers —; and (c) below the European mean in terms of efficiency — the system should be doing better when the investment and the sociocultural level of parents is taken into account. Notwithstanding, it should be noticed that

(i) Catalonia's results are quite similar but higher than those of Spain as a whole, and (ii) the large percentage of recently arrived foreign pupils has a noticeable negative impact on global results. In other words, in global terms, while the general results may not be satisfactory enough for a society that takes pride in its long pedagogical tradition, Catalonia's educational system seems to be doing at least as well as the Spanish system. That is to say the adoption of Catalan as the predominant school language is not proving detrimental to the educational outcomes as a whole. And this is particularly significant taking into account that the percentage of new immigrant population is much higher in the Catalan-speaking territories than in most of Castilian-speaking Spain.

A summary — and some challenges

Language policies in the Catalan language area have evolved dramatically during the last decades due to two factors. On the one hand, the legal and political reorganization of the nation-states has resulted in some capacity of self-organization in the Catalan-speaking societies; on the other, the global ideological evolution has reduced the State's power to impose specific language policies. The position of Catalan has benefitted from both circumstances, and it is today much stronger than it used to be.

The different societies where Catalan is the historical language have developed quite different language-in-education policies and models. Some territories have opted for integrated schools, while others have chosen systems based on language streams or even independent educational systems. In general terms, it is only in systems where Catalan has a significant role as a means of instruction where non-native speakers manage to learn it. On the contrary, the state languages have achieved such a hegemonic social position in the Catalan-speaking territories that seem to be learned thoroughly even when they are not the predominant means of instruction.

The educational systems in the Catalan-speaking areas face a number of challenges. In terms of language competence, they have to keep proving their ability to obtain high levels of bilingual competence, and find a way to convert this bilingual competence into a trilingual or even quadrilingual repertoire. Some of the systems here reviewed — such as the Andorran school — are already approaching that goal. Others — such as the Castilian medium schools in Valencia — still have to pass from monolingualism to bilingualism. In terms of language practices, the educational systems here reviewed should learn how to encourage the use of the historically minoritised language in a liberal, pluralistic environment. Again, some systems such as La Bressola may be suggesting a way. Third, in non-linguistic terms, all these systems face the challenge of proving that bilingual schools may be at least as successful as monolingual schools in guaranteeing equitable and excellent education for as many as possible. Small networks of schools may find this easier than larger systems, but the challenge is there for all of them. Fourth, most of these systems were created in a *traditional* bilingual context where the historical language had to deal with the pressure of the state language. Today, these very systems have to adapt to a new multilingual, multicultural environment, where immigrant languages combine with globalization. Finally, most of these systems are regarded with suspicion by many majority speakers, especially those living in traditionally monolingual areas. This is an unfortunate situation in a moment in which Europe is progressing towards multilingualism and multiculturalism. The experience in dealing with sustainable multilingualism of the schools here analyzed could become a valuable contribution to progress in the direction of a more pluralistic European society. Their main actors should make an effort to make this contribution known beyond their borders, an effort that may eventually turn out to be beneficial for their systems as well.

Acknowledgement

This article is supported by the Spanish Ministry of Science and Innovation research grant HUM2006-05860.

Notes

1. Order of 30 June 1998. DOGV [Official Journal of the Valencian *Generalitat*] 3285, of 14 July. http://www.ua.es/uem/legislacio/ordre300698.html.

2. Resolution of 1 October 1985, of the Ministry of Education and Science, which publishes the agreement on the teaching of Catalan in the eastern strip of Aragon.

3. Otherwise said, data in this section come from Pons and Sorolla *in press*.

4. http://bressola.cat/, last visit 29 October 2008

5. Parents in Spain can choose between public education, i.e., run by the public authorities; subsidised private education (*escuela concertada*); and non-subsidised private education. The first two categories, which serve almost all students, are in theory free of charge. Nevertheless, most subsidised private schools usually charge some extra mensual fees, which makes them less accessible for low-income families.

6. See this and other initiatives at. http://www.xtec.cat/lic/documents.htm

References

Acadèmia Valenciana de la Llengua. 2005. *Llibre blanc de l'ús del valencià — I. Enquesta sobre la situació social del valencià. 2004*. València: Acadèmia Valenciana de la Llengua. Available online: http://www.avl.gva.es/img/EdicionsPublicacions/Publicacions/Blanc.pdf.
Alturo, N. & Vila, F.X. (eds). 2002. *Variació dialectal i estandardització*. Barcelona: PPU; Secció de Lingüística Catalana, Departament de Filologia Catalana, Universitat de Barcelona.

Areny, M. 2002. Directrius en relació amb l'estandardització i la diversitat dialectal en l'ensenyament infantil i primari a Catalunya. In *Variació dialectal i estandardització,* N. Alturo & F. X. Vila (eds), 99–108. Barcelona: PPU; Secció de Lingüística Catalana, Departament de Filologia Catalana, Universitat de Barcelona.

Arnau, J. 2004. Sobre les competències en català i castellà dels escolars de Catalunya: Una resposta a la polèmica sobre el decret d'hores de castellà. *LSC — Llengua Societat i Comunicació* 1:1–7. http://www.ub.edu/cusc/LSC_set.htm.

Baldaquí i Escandell, J.M. 2006. *El model de llengua i la seguretat lingüística dels jóvens valencians.* València; Barcelona: Institut Interuniversitari de Filologia Valenciana; Publicacions de l'Abadia de Montserrat.

Bastardas i Boada, A. 1985. *La bilingüització de la segona generació immigrant. Realitat i factors a Vilafranca del Penedès.* Barcelona: La Magrana.

Bastardas i Boada, A. 1986. *Llengua i immigració. La segona generació immigrant a la Catalunya no metropolitana.* Barcelona: La Magrana.

Becat, J. 2000. *La situació del català a França. Aspectes jurídics i docents i estudis sobre la matèria.* Barcelona: Institut d'Estudis Catalans.

Boix-Fuster, E. 1990. Language choice and language switching among young people in Barcelona: Concepts, methods and data. In *Network on Code Switching and Language Contact-Basel,* 209–226 Strasbourg: European Science Foundation.

Carrera-Sabaté, J. 2002. *Escola catalana i variació fonètica. Una evolució del vocalisme àton a Alguaire i a Lleida.* Lleida: Pagès.

Chessa, E. 2007. *Estadística sobre els usos lingüístics a l'Alguer: llengua i societat a l'Alguer en els inicis del segle XXI.* Barcelona: Generalitat de Catalunya, Departament de Presidència.

CSASE Consell Superior d'Avaluació del Sistema Educatiu. 2007. *Sistema d'Indicadors d'Educació de Catalunya.* Barcelona: Consell Superior d'Avaluació del Sistema Educatiu.

CSASE Consell Superior d'Avaluació del Sistema Educatiu. 2008. *Avaluació de l'educació secundària obligatòria 2006: Estudi sociodemogràfic i lingüístic als centres d'educació secundària de Catalunya..* Barcelona: Generalitat de Catalunya, Departament d'Educació.

De Melchor, V. & Branchadell, A. 2002. *El catalán. Una lengua de Europa para compartir.* Bellaterra: Servei de Publicacions de la Universitat Autònoma de Barcelona.

Ferrando, A. & Nicolás, M. 1993. *Panorama d'història de la llengua.* València: Tàndem.

Ferrer, F. (dir.), Valiente, Ò. & Castel, J.L. 2008. Equitat, excel·lència i eficiència educativa a Catalunya. Una anàlisi comparada. Avançament de resultats (I). Dossier de premsa. Fundació Jaume Bofill, Barcelona. Available online: http://www.fbofill.cat/?codmenu=01&not=254

Ferrer i Gironès, F. 1985. *La persecució política de la llengua catalana. Història de les mesures preses contra el seu ús des de la Nova Planta fins avui.* Barcelona: Ed. 62.

Galindo, M. 2006. Les llengües a l'hora del pati. Usos lingüístics en les converses dels infants de primària a Catalunya. PhD dissertation, Universitat de Barcelona.

Galindo Solé, M. with. F. X. Vila i Moreno's collaboration. 2008. *Les llengües en joc, el joc de les llengües. L'ús interpersonal del català entre els infants i joves de Catalunya.* Lleida: Pagès editors.

Gomàriz i Auró, E. In press. Els usos lingüístics interpersonals dins i fora de la llar de l'alumnat autòcton i immigrant de sisè d'educació primària de Vic. *Interlingüística* 18.

Guinot, E.. 1999. *Els fundadors del Regne de València,* València: Tres i Quatre.

Hall, J.. 2001. *Convivència in Catalonia: Languages Living Together:* Fundació Jaume Bofill.

La Bressola. 2007. *La realitat d'un somni. Trenta anys d'escoles catalanes a la Catalunya del nord.* Barcelona: Edicions de 1984.

Pons, E. & Vila i Moreno, F.X. 2005. *Informe sobre la situació de la llengua catalana (2003–2004)*. Barcelona: Observatori de la Llengua. Available online: http://www.observatoridelallengua. org/arxius_documents/informe6_ok.pdf

Pons, E. & Sorolla Vidal, N. In press. *Informe de la llengua catalana (2005–2007)*. Barcelona: Institut d'Estudis Catalans.

Pueyo, M. 1996. *Tres escoles per als catalans*. Lleida: Pagès editors.

Purtí, E. 2006. La incorporació tardana de l'alumnat al·loglot. L'experiència dels primers programes adreçats a l'alumnat extracomunitaris a Cataunya. In *Integrar, des de la fragilitat? Societats plurilingües davant els reptes de les immigracions multilingües: Suïssa, Brussel·les, Luxemburg, Quebec i Catalunya*, F. X. Vila i Moreno, E. Boix-Fuster & N. Alturo (eds), 83–87. Barcelona: Institut d'Estudis Catalans.

Querol Puig, E. (coord.), Chessa, E., Sorolla, N., Torres i Pla, J, with collaboration of Sanjuán, X. & Solís, M. 2007. *Llengua i societat als territoris de parla catalana a l'inici del segle XXI. L'Alguer, Andorra, Catalunya, Catalunya Nord; la Franja, Illes Balears i Comunitat Valenciana*. Barcelona: Generalitat de Catalunya, Departament de Vicepresidència, Secretaria de Política Lingüística.

Spolsky, B. 2004. *Language Policy*. Cambridge: CUP.

Síndic — El defensor de les persones. 2008. La segregació escolar a Catalunya. Informe extraordinari, maig 2008. Síndic de Greuges, Barcelona. Available at: https://www.sindic.cat/site/ unitFiles/2266/60_INFORME%20SEGREGACIO%20ESCOLAR.pdf

Torres, J. (coord.), Vila i Moreno, F.X., Fabà, A., Bretxa i Riera, V., Sorolla, N. & Pradilla, M. À. 2006. *Enquesta sobre els usos lingüístics a Andorra 2004. Llengua i societat a Andorra en els inicis del segle XXI*. Barcelona: Generalitat de Catalunya, Departament de la Vicepresidència, Secretaria General de Política Lingüística.

Unamuno, V. 1997. Lenguas, identidades y escuela: Etnografía de la acción comunicativa. PhD dissertation, Universitat Autònoma de Barcelona.

Vila i Moreno, F.X. 2005. 2. Els coneixements lingüístics. In *Estadística sobre els usos lingüístics a Catalunya 2003. Llengua i societat a Catalunya en els inicis del segle XXI*, J. Torres (coord.), F.X. Vila i Moreno, A. Fabà & V. Bretxa i Riera, 17–54. Barcelona: Secretaria General de Política Lingüística, Generalitat de Catalunya.

Vila i Moreno, F.X.. 2008. Catalan in Spain. In *Multilingual Europe: Facts and Policies*, G. Extra & D. Gorter (eds), 157–183. Berlin: Mouton de Gruyter.

Vila i Moreno, F.X., Vial i Rius, S. & Galindo, M. 2005. Language practices in bilingual schools: Some observed, quantitative data from Catalonia. In *Bilingualism and Education: From the Family to the School*, X.P. Rodríguez-Yáñez, A.M. Lorenzo Suárez & F. Ramallo (eds), 263–273. Munich: Lincom.

Author's address

F. Xavier Vila i Moreno
Centre Universitari de Sociolingüística i Comunicació –
Universitat de Barcelona / Parc Científic de Barcelona
CRUSCAT network — Institut d'Estudis Catalans

fxvila@ub.edu

The declining role of primary schools in the revitalisation of Irish

John Harris
Trinity College, Dublin

Although the vast majority of people in Ireland have at least some knowledge of Irish, only a small minority speak it as a community language (in Gaeltacht areas in the west) or in the more widely dispersed Irish-speaking households in the large English speaking area. Primary schools have had a central role in language revitalisation since the late 19th century, by transmitting a knowledge of the language to each new generation. This paper examines how well primary schools have performed in recent decades. Results of a national comparative study over a 17 year period show that there has been a long-term decline in pupil success in learning Irish (speaking and listening) in 'ordinary' schools. Proficiency in Irish in all-Irish immersion schools in English-speaking areas have held up well despite rapid expansion. Reasons for the decline in ordinary schools include time pressures in the curriculum, a reduction in Irish-medium teaching, changing teacher attitudes and a lack of engagement by parents. The changing role of the Department of Education and Science in relation to Irish and the rapid evolution of new educational structures, have also have had negative effects. Implications for the revitalisation of Irish are discussed.

Introduction

Irish is spoken as a community and home language only in relatively small ('Gaeltacht') areas, mainly along the west coast of Ireland. Despite its minority status in terms of number of speakers, it has been the first official language of the Republic of Ireland since early in the life of the new state. As a result of the widespread teaching of the language at primary and post-primary levels in the intervening 85 years, a substantial proportion of the population can now speak it (1.66 million according to the 2006 census). Actual use of Irish for day to day communication outside the Gaeltacht heartland, however, is not common. The contribution of the education system is crucial to compensating for the failure of natural transmission of the language within families outside these core areas. In the vast majority of cases, Irish is taught as a sec-

AILA Review 21 (2008), **49–68**. DOI 10.1075/aila.21.05har
ISSN 1461–0213 / E-ISSN 1570–5595 © John Benjamins Publishing Company

ond language to English speaking children, who learn it as one subject in 'ordinary' mainstream schools. It is also taught in immersion ('all-Irish') schools which, while still relatively small in number, have grown substantially over the last twenty years. In addition, of course, it is taught in Gaeltacht schools.

The Irish language planning and revitalisation experiment has provided a key case study for scholars working on topics such as language endangerment and and reversing language shift (Dorian, 1988; Fishman, 1991, 2001; Macnamara, 1971; Ó Riagáin, 2001; Spolsky, 2004; Wright, 2004). Three features together distinguish the Irish initiative from other well known cases of language planning and revitalisation: (1) the weak position of the language in the Gaeltacht Irish-speaking areas in the west at the time when the state initiative originally began in 1922; (2) the failure in the interim to improve the rate of intergenerational transmission of the language within families and homes — either in the Gaeltacht, or in the country more generally; (3) and the heavy reliance placed on the education system to reproduce a basic competence in the language in each new generation.

Primary schools have been central to the fortunes of Irish, both positively and negatively, since the early 19th century. An extensive network of national schools established in 1831 under the Commissioners of Education had grown by the end of the century to 8600 national schools attended by over three quarters of a million children. It was not until 1878, however, that Irish was included in the national curriculum. Even then, it was included only as a marginal extra subject, despite the fact that it was a vernacular and only language for a significant segment of the population (almost 320 thousand in 1851) (Ó Buachalla, 1984). Following independence, primary schools were again a major focus, this time as the central plank of the new state's efforts to promote the language. By 1941, 12.3% of primary schools were teaching entirely through Irish, while a further 43.2% were teaching varying proportions of children through the language (Ó Buachalla, 1984, 1988; Ó Riagáin, 1997). Subsequently, this programme contracted significantly again, however, so that by 1980/1981 only 3% of children nationally, including those in Gaeltacht areas, were being taught entirely through Irish (Ó Domhnalláin,1987; Ó Riagáin, 1997). Arguably, one of the factors which accelerated this decline was the publication of John Macnamara's major 1966 study of the impact of Irish-medium education for English speaking children (Macnamara, 1966). Ó Buachalla (1984) estimates that in 1984, there were only 23 all-Irish schools outside Gaeltacht areas, with a total enrollement of only 3389 pupils. Since the early 1980s, the all-Irish sector has once again grown rapidly from this small base (Harris et al, 2006), this time on the initiative of parents rather than Government.

The present paper analyses the performance of ordinary and all-Irish (immersion) primary schools in recent decades, mainly from the point of view of their contribution to language revitalisation outside Gaeltacht areas. Our focus is on the success or otherwise of schools in developing pupil proficiency in the language. Much of the discussion centres around a major study which tried to establish long-term trends in standards in the period between the mid 1980s and 2002. The data derive from objective tests administered to national samples of schools by external examiners. Data on teachers' and parents' views and practices are also presented. We begin however with an examination of the performance of primary schools nationally in the twenty year period immediately preceding that study.

1960s–1980s: Relative stability in Irish proficiency

Two different kinds of data on standards of achievement in Irish in this era are available. The judgements of teachers and principals nationally provide information for the earlier part of this period, while national assessments based on objective tests of Irish Listening and Irish Speaking provide data on the later part. Three studies conducted in the mid 1970s were based on the perceptions of primary schools teachers. In one of these a national sample of teachers between the ages of 35 and 55 was asked to compare the general standard of proficiency in Irish of pupils completing fifth and sixth grade at that time with the standard achieved ten years earlier (in the mid 1960s). More teachers in the mid 1970s thought that standards were worse (48%) than thought they were better (39%), while 13% thought they were unchanged (Ó Domhnalláin and Ó Gliasáin, 1976). The Irish National Teachers Organisation, in a national survey of members in 1976, asked about standards attained during the previous five years. Slightly more teachers thought that standards in oral Irish has declined (42%) than thought they had improved (36%), while 14% perceived no change and 8% had no opinion.

Standards in Irish spelling and, to a lesser extent in Irish writing were also perceived by more teachers to have declined than to have improved. Standards of Irish reading, however, were seen by more teachers as improving than declining (19%) (Irish National Teachers' Organisation, 1976).

In a survey conducted by the Government Department of Education at about the same time, primary school principals were asked to record the perceptions of senior and junior school teachers. At junior level, more teachers thought standards in oral Irish had improved (51%) than thought they had declined (31%). At senior level, however, slightly more teachers thought standards in oral Irish had declined (38%) than thought they had improved. Most teachers at both junior (72%) and senior (69%) levels perceived standards of Irish reading as having improved. Standards of creative and functional writing in Irish were also seen as having improved, while the presentation of written work was thought to have declined (Fontes and Kellaghan, 1977).

Two factors need to be taken into account in drawing general conclusions from these three studies. First, one of them deals with senior primary grades only, a second deals with all primary grades together, while the third deals separately with senior and junior primary grades. Second, evidence for an overall decline or improvement in standards should be based on the magnitude and direction of the difference between the percentage of teachers who perceived an improvement and the percentage who perceived a decline. Bearing these points in mind, it seems that, on balance, teachers perceived a relatively small decline in standards of oral Irish or general proficiency in Irish at senior grades, but an improvement at junior grades. Irish reading was perceived as having improved at both senior and junior grades. Irish spelling was perceived as having declined, while the situation regarding writing is unclear. At the time the studies were published and subsequently, however, statistics from these three studies were sometimes quoted out of context as evidence for a dramatic decline in standards of achievement in Irish (Harris, 1984). What was often ignored was that the percentage of teachers perceiving an improvement in performance or perceiving no change was quite substantial.

Another source of evidence on standards of achievement in Irish in this period is a series of national surveys conducted in the late 1970s to the mid 1980s by Institiúid Teangeolaíochta Éireann (Harris, 1982, 1983, 1984, 1988, 1997; Harris and Murtagh, 1988b). These showed that about one-third of pupils in ordinary schools attained mastery of each of a number of curricular objectives in Irish (Listening and Speaking) at sixth, fourth, and second grade. Criterion-referenced tests, based on the *Nuachúrsaí*, the official Department of Education audio-visual conversation courses in Irish for primary schools (Department of Education, 1978), were used.

The relatively small proportions attaining mastery of objectives at each grade, however, indicated that there was a very substantial gap between the level of performance in spoken Irish, which the *Nuachúrsaí* aimed at, and the level attained by most pupils (Harris, 1984). It was argued that the gap was primarily due to unrealistic performance expectations rather than to factors such as inadequate teaching or unsuitable courses and methods. This conclusion was based on comparisons between the achievement in spoken Irish of pupils who learned Irish simply as a subject with a variety of other groups who might be described as linguistically or educationally advantaged in relation to Irish (Harris, 1984). A comparison of the results of these surveys in 1978 and 1985, however, revealed a modest but statistically significant increase in the percentage of pupils in ordinary primary schools achieving mastery of each of the sixth-grade objectives in Irish over the seven-year period (Harris and Murtagh, 1988b).

Mid 1980s–2002: A dramatic decline in Irish at primary level

We turn now to the study which is the main focus of this paper. This is a national survey of achievement in spoken Irish in 'ordinary', 'all-Irish' and Gaeltacht schools, conducted in 2002 (Harris et al 2006). The results of this are compared with a corresponding study carried out 17 years earlier in 1985 (Harris and Murtagh, 1988b described in the previous section). Although the two surveys examined *both* Irish Listening and Irish Speaking skills in all *three* kinds of schools, most of the analyses here will be confined to Irish Listening and to pupils in ordinary and all-Irish schools outside Gaeltacht areas.

The surveys and tests

A number of minor but essential changes had to be made in the original 1985 tests of Irish Listening and Irish Speaking for the 2002 administration. These were necessary in order to accommodate changes in culture or in the physical environment in the interim (e.g. the changeover from the pound to the euro and changes in house furnishings). These modifications were made in such a way that the basic linguistic content of the items was not altered in any fundamental way. A number of statistical checks were made to establish the test was not any more difficult for pupils in 2002 because of these adjustments (see Harris et al, 2006).

Most of the Irish proficiency data generated by these surveys consist of the percentage of sixth-grade pupils who achieve each of three defined levels of performance on each of the content-skill objectives in Irish Listening and Irish Speaking represented on the test: (i) mastery (a high level of performance), (ii) at least minimal progress (without attaining mastery), and (iii) failure. The analysis reported below is based on 'mastery' and 'failure'. We also compare overall mean scores on the tests in 1985 and 2002.

Seven content-skill objectives were represented on the Irish Listening Test and they are identified here by brief names such as *Listening vocabulary*. A greater number of items on the test are devoted to the more general objectives e.g. *General comprehension of speech*. Fewer items are assigned to objectives which require pupils to identify the correct *form* of a particular Irish word to fit a given spoken or pictorial context (e.g.*Understanding the morphology of verbs in listening*). All items were in multiple-choice form and were presented on audio tape to entire class-groups of pupils. Examiners could give instructions in Irish or English, whichever language would best ensure that the pupil understood the task. The items themselves, however, were entirely in Irish.

Changes in Irish proficiency in ordinary schools over 17 years

Whether we examine overall mean scores or the percentages of pupils attaining mastery of individual objectives, it is clear that there has been a considerable drop between 1985 and 2002 in performance in Irish Listening in ordinary schools. The fall in mean score in ordinary schools (Table 1) amounts to 12.9 raw score points, almost the 1985 standard deviation. There is no significant difference between mean scores in Irish Listening in 1985 and 2002 in the case of all-Irish and Gaeltacht schools.

In addition, there has been a substantial and statistically significant fall-off between 1985 and 2002 in the percentage of pupils in ordinary schools attaining high levels of performance (mastery) for six of the seven Irish Listening objectives tested (Table 2). For example, there was a fall of 36.1% and 40.5% respectively in the percentages of pupils mastering the *Listening vocabulary* and *General comprehension of speech* objectives.

Table 1. Mean raw scores of pupils on the Irish Listening Test in 1985 and 2002 in ordinary, all-Irish, and Gaeltacht schools.

School type	1985 Mean (SE)	Standard deviation	2002 Mean (SE)	Standard deviation	Difference 2002–1985
Ordinary	46.9 *(0.97)*	13.65	34.0 *(0.47)*	9.35	**−12.9**
All-Irish	66.0 *(1.09)*	6.95	63.7 *(0.71)*	6.56	− 2.3
Gaeltacht	59.8 *(1.46)*	11.23	56.1 *(1.80)*	13.72	− 3.7

Significant differences ($p < .05$) are printed in bold. Standard errors are printed in italics.

Table 2. Percentage of sixth-grade pupils in ordinary schools who attain mastery on each objective on the Irish Listening Test in 1985 and 2002.

Ordinary Schools Listening objective	Attain mastery 1985	2002	Difference (2002–1985)
Sound discrimination	84.7% *(1.39)*	84.2% *(1.41)*	− 0.5%
Listening vocabulary	42.0% *(3.00)*	5.9% *(1.08)*	**−36.1%**
General comprehension of speech	48.3% *(2.94)*	7.8% *(1.20)*	**−40.5%**
Understanding the morphology of verbs	26.9% *(2.35)*	2.9% *(0.61)*	**−24.0%**
Understanding the morphology of prepositions	33.9% *(2.43)*	11.8% *(0.91)*	**−22.1%**
Understanding the morphology of qualifiers	30.6% *(2.68)*	14.0% *(1.42)*	**−16.6%**
Understanding the morphology of nouns	16.8% *(1.54)*	3.7% *(0.49)*	**−13.1%**

Significant differences ($p < .05$) are printed in bold. Standard error printed in italics. N (1985) = 2155, N (2002) = 2728.

The result is that only 5.9% and 7.8% of pupils respectively in ordinary schools achieve mastery of these two objectives in 2002. The decline in relation to these objectives would seem to be of particular importance because they are central to the use of Irish for real communication.

Objectives relating to *Understanding the morphology of verbs in listening* and *Understanding the morphology of prepositions in listening* are associated with falls of 24% and 22.1% respectively, with only 2.9% and 11.8% respectively still mastering these objectives in 2002. Two other objectives, related to understanding the morphology of qualifiers and nouns are associated with a decline in the percentage achieving mastery of 16.6% and 13.1% respectively. *Sound discrimination* is the only objective where the decline in performance is not statistically significant.

For most objectives, the decline in the percentage of pupils in ordinary schools attaining mastery is associated with a moderate increase in the percentage of pupils reaching the lower level of performance defined as 'minimal progress', but a larger increase in the percentages failing. For example, *Listening vocabulary* and *General comprehension of speech* are associated with an increase, between 1985 and 2002, of 27.9% and 24.4% respectively in the percentages 'failing' (Table 3), while increases in the percentages making 'at least minimal progress' (not shown in tabular form) are only 8.3% and 16% respectively.

Table 3. Percentage of sixth-grade pupils in ordinary schools who fail each objective on the Irish Listening Test in 1985 and 2002.

Ordinary Schools Listening objective	Fail		Difference
	1985	2002	(2002–1985)
Sound discrimination	3.9% *(0.53)*	3.1% *(0.66)*	– 0.8%
Listening vocabulary	14.4% *(1.93)*	42.3% *(2.00)*	**+27.9%**
General comprehension of speech	11.8% *(1.59)*	36.2% *(1.75)*	**+24.4%**
Understanding the morphology of verbs	27.7% *(2.00)*	48.7% *(1.40)*	**+21.0%**
Understanding the morphology of prepositions	9.6% *(0.93)*	18.9% *(1.09)*	**+ 9.3%**
Understanding the morphology of qualifiers	15.7% *(1.42)*	23.3% *(1.22)*	**+ 7.6%**
Understanding the morphology of nouns	19.7% *(1.54)*	37.5% *(1.54)*	**+17.8%**

Significant differences ($p < .05$) are printed in bold. Standard error printed in italics. N (1985) = 2155, N (2002) = 2728.

Changes in Irish proficiency in all-Irish schools

Turning to all-Irish schools, we found that very high percentages of pupils achieved mastery of most objectives in 2002 (Table 4). *Listening vocabulary* and *General comprehension of speech*, for example, are mastered by 89.3% and 96.3% respectively.

In the case of a further three objectives, the lowest percentage attaining mastery is 86.4%. Despite the generally high percentages of all-Irish pupils mastering most Irish Listening objectives in 2002, and the fact that overall mean score on the test in 1985 and 2002 do not differ significantly (Table 1), there are statistically significant declines since 1985 in the percentage of pupils mastering three objectives — *Understanding the morphology of verbs in listening* (a fall of 14.8%), Understanding *the morphology of prepositions in listening* (a decline of 6.6%) and *Understanding the morphology of nouns* (a fall of 24.4%).

Table 4. Percentage of sixth-grade pupils in all-Irish schools who attain mastery on each objective on the Irish Listening Test in 1985 and 2002.

All-Irish Schools Listening objective	Attain mastery		Difference
	1985	2002	(2002–1985)
Sound discrimination	96.0% *(1.24)*	97.0% *(1.06)*	+ 1.0%
Listening vocabulary	90.4% *(4.04)*	89.3% *(3.13)*	– 1.1%
General comprehension of speech	96.4% *(1.00)*	96.3% *(1.92)*	– 0.1%
Understanding the morphology of verbs	76.1% *(3.72)*	61.3% *(4.02)*	**−14.8%**
Understanding the morphology of prepositions	93.0% *(1.44)*	86.4% *(1.57)*	**– 6.6%**
Understanding the morphology of qualifiers	80.1% *(2.69)*	87.8% *(2.12)*	+ 7.7%
Understanding the morphology of nouns	56.5% *(6.89)*	32.1% *(3.06)*	**−24.4%**

Significant differences ($p < .05$) are printed in bold. Standard error printed in italics. N (1985) = 301, N = 640 (2002)

Unlike the situation in ordinary schools, the decline in the percentages attaining mastery of specific objectives in all-Irish schools involves a slippage to minimal progress rather than to failure (latter results not shown in tabular form). Failure on all of the seven listening objectives is extremely low in all-Irish schools, and in all but one case *Understanding the morphology of qualifiers in listening* (where the increase is only 0.3%), has not changed significantly since 1985

It should be noted also (Table 4) that the two central Irish Listening objectives, *Listening vocabulary* and *General comprehension of speech,* are mastered by very similar percentages of all-Irish pupils in 1985 and 2002 and the differences are not statistically significant. These latter objectives are also the ones tested by the greatest number of items. Finally, in this regard, the percentage of pupils in all-Irish schools attaining mastery of one Irish Listening objective, *Understanding the morphology of qualifiers,* actually *increased* significantly (by 7.7%) between 1985 and 2002. A further objective *Sound discrimination* is also associated with an increase in the percentage attaining mastery in 2002, but this is not statistically significant.

Perhaps the most important aspect of the all-Irish school results is that they show that all-Irish schools have maintained generally high standards of pupil achievement in Irish — standards which are overwhelming superior to ordinary schools — during a period when the all-Irish sector increased from 1.1% of pupils to more than 5% nationally. In effect, we are examining the performance of a school sector which is now considerably more mainstream in composition of pupils than it was in the mid 1980s. Very likely the 2002 population differs quite substantially in terms of knowledge and use of Irish at home (Harris et al 2006).

Overall mean scores on Irish Listening for all-Irish schools do not differ significantly between the two years.

Long-term changes in teachers' attitudes

We turn now to some of the findings of the surveys of teachers and parents. These data will be useful later in considering some of the factors which may be responsible for the decline in achievement in Irish in ordinary schools. We begin with 2002 data on teachers' views on standards of speaking proficiency in Irish over a 15-year period (or since the teacher began teaching). A large majority of pupils in ordinary schools (76.6%) were taught by teachers who believed that the standard of speaking proficiency of pupils had declined, while only 5.3% had teachers who believed standards had improved. These results are in sharp contrast with the results of the three national surveys carried out in the 1970s mentioned earlier in the paper, where the proportions of teachers perceiving a decline and an improvement were much more evenly balanced. We also found that the 2002 judgements of all-Irish school teachers much more closely resemble the pattern of teacher surveys in the 1970s. That is, in all-Irish schools the percentages of pupils who have teachers perceiving a decline in speaking proficiency (29.3%) and perceiving an improvement (27.0%) are roughly equal. Thus, both ordinary and all-Irish school teachers' judgements of changes in standards in the 1985–2002 period match the results of the objective tests of proficiency.

Data in Table 5 show that the vast majority of sixth-grade pupils in ordinary schools had teachers whose attitudes to Irish were either 'very' favourable (36.2%) or 'favourable' (51.4%). Only 5% of pupils were taught by teachers whose attitudes were unfavourable or very unfavourable. As we will see later (Table 8), ordinary school parents in general have less favourable attitudes than teachers.

The percentage of pupils in all-Irish schools whose teachers had favourable attitudes exceeds the percentage in ordinary schools, and no pupil in an all-Irish school had a teacher whose attitude was either neutral or unfavourable. The percentage who judged themselves to be 'very favourable' is also much higher than in ordinary schools.

Table 6 presents data on teachers' attitude to Irish being taught in ordinary schools in 1985 and 2002. Basically, in 2002 large majorities of pupils (81.3%) have teachers who are favourable or very favourable. There has, however, been a statistically significant fall of 8.9% (from 90.2%) since 1985 in the percentage whose teachers were favourable. All pupils in Gaeltacht and all-Irish schools in 2002 had teachers whose attitude to Irish being taught in school was favourable or very favourable.

Table 5. Percentage of sixth-grade pupils in ordinary and all-Irish schools according to their teachers' own attitude to Irish.

Teachers' own Attitude to Irish	Percentage (SE) of pupils	
	Ordinary	All-Irish
Very Favourable	36.2% (3.30)	88.2% (6.94)
Favourable	51.4% (3.74)	11.8% (6.94)
Neutral	6.6% (2.23)	0%
Unfavourable	4.4% (1.68)	0%
Very unfavourable	0.6% (0.62)	0%
Missing	0.7% (0.72)	0%

Standard error printed in italics. N Ordinary = 3037, N All-Irish = 683.

Table 6. Percentage of sixth-grade pupils in ordinary schools according to their teachers' attitude to Irish being taught in primary schools: Comparison of 1985 and 2002.

Teachers' attitude to Irish being taught to pupils in primary school	Percentage (SE) of pupils		Difference (2002–1985)
	1985	2002	
Very Favourable/Favourable	90.2% (3.19)	81.3% (2.85)	**−8.9%**
Neutral	6.2% (2.52)	12.5% (2.90)	**+6.3%**
Unfavourable/Very unfavourable	3.6% (2.07)	5.5% (1.95)	+1.9%
Missing	0%	0.7% (0.72)	+0.7%

Significant differences (p < .05) are printed in bold. Standard error printed in italics. N (1985) = 2060, N (2002) = 3037

Table 7. Percentage of sixth-grade pupils in ordinary schools according to the satisfaction derived by their teacher from teaching Irish: 1985 and 2002.

Satisfaction derived by teacher from teaching Irish	Percentage (*SE*) of pupils		Difference (2002–1985)
	1985	2002	
Great satisfaction/Satisfaction	80.3% (*4.90*)	55.4% (*3.81*)	**−24.9%**
Neutral	10.7% (*3.67*)	18.5% (*3.18*)	+ 7.8%
Dissatisfaction/Great dissatisfaction	9.0% (*3.25*)	24.6% (*3.45*)	**+15.6%**
Missing	0%	1.5% (*1.08*)	+ 1.5%

Significant differences ($p < .05$) are printed in bold. Standard error printed in italics. N (1985) = 2060, N (2002) = 3037.

The percentage of pupils in ordinary schools whose teachers derived satisfaction from teaching Irish, had fallen by a considerable amount (Table 7). While 80.3% of pupils had teachers who derived satisfaction or great satisfaction from teaching Irish in 1985, only 55.4% had in 2002. Correspondingly, the percentage whose teachers reported dissatisfaction or great dissatisfaction had risen by 15.6%. The percentage whose teachers represented themselves as 'neutral' on the question of satisfaction had also risen by 7.8%, although this change is not statistically significant. These relatively low levels of satisfaction are almost entirely confined to ordinary schools. In 2002, for example, no pupil in an all-Irish school, and only 6.6% of pupils in Gaeltacht schools, was taught by a teacher who expressed *dissatisfaction* with teaching Irish (data not shown in tabular form). Previous studies have shown that teacher satisfaction in teaching Irish is significantly linked to pupil achievement in spoken Irish.

Parents and Irish: Attitudes, speech to children and encouragement

We turn now to data on a few key issues relating to parents. All these data relate to 2002, as we do not have corresponding data for 1985. In answer to a question which asked 'What is your general attitude to Irish now?', the most common response of parents of pupils in ordinary schools was 'neutral' (39.6%), followed closely by 'favourable' (34.2%) (Table 8). Smaller percentages were 'very favourable', 'unfavourable' or 'very unfavourable'. The contrast with the attitudes of all-Irish school parents is striking: 56.5% of all-Irish parents were very favourable towards Irish, compared to 14.5% of ordinary school parents. Note also the contrast between the attitudes of ordinary school parents here and those of teachers earlier (Table 5) where 36.2% were 'very' favourable and another 51.4% were 'favourable'.

The most frequent *speaking ability* category selected by parents to describe themselves (Table 9) varies by school type. 'A few simple sentences' is the most frequent category in the case of ordinary school parents (37.7%), while 'parts of conversations' is the description most often chosen by all-Irish school parents (38.3%). A combined total of 32% of ordinary school parents assign themselves to one of the two lowest

Table 8. Percentage of parents in ordinary and all-Irish schools according to their general attitude to Irish now.

Parents' general attitude to Irish now	Ordinary	All-Irish
Very Favourable	14.5% *(0.71)*	56.5% *(3.12)*
Favourable	34.2% *(0.97)*	35.9% *(2.56)*
Neutral	39.6% *(0.96)*	6.6% *(0.98)*
Unfavourable/Very unfavourable	11.2% *(0.67)*	0.7% *(0.35)*
Missing	0.5% *(0.13)*	0.3% *(0.22)*

Standard error printed in italics. N Ordinary = 2744, N All-Irish = 609.

Table 9. Percentage of parents in ordinary and all-Irish schools according to their self-assessed ability to speak Irish.

Parents' ability to speak Irish	Ordinary	All-Irish
No Irish	10.8% *(0.89)*	1.8% *(0.64)*
Only the odd word	21.2% *(0.97)*	8.2% *(1.30)*
A few simple sentences	37.7% *(1.18)*	26.9% *(1.65)*
Parts of conversation	22.6% *(1.00)*	38.3% *(2.44)*
Most conversations	6.2% *(0.51)*	18.7% *(1.90)*
Native speaker ability	1.0% *(0.18)*	5.8% *(1.17)*
Missing	0.6% *(0.14)*	0.4% *(0.24)*

Standard error printed in italics. N Ordinary = 2744, N All-Irish = 609

Irish-speaking categories: 'No Irish' and 'the odd word'. By comparison with ordinary school parents, only 10% of all-Irish parents rated their speaking ability as low as 'no Irish' or 'only the odd word'.

Substantial percentages of parents of pupils in ordinary schools rarely if ever speak Irish to their children (33.1% 'seldom' and 42.3% 'never') (Table 10). All-Irish school parents do not fall into these low usage patterns as often: while 25.5% of them 'seldom' speak Irish to the child, only 8.4% 'never' do.

Parents were also asked what general attitude to Irish they try to encourage in their child (Table 11). All-Irish schools parents chose the option 'I let my child know that Irish is important' in 55% of cases, while those in ordinary schools chose it in 32.5% of cases. Two-thirds of ordinary school parents, however, say 'I leave it up to my child to develop his/her own attitude to Irish'.

Gaeltacht parents (not shown here) were the most affirmative of all, with 64.2% choosing the option 'I let my child know that Irish is important'.

Finally, previous work (Harris and Murtagh, 1999) has shown that another element of parental support for Irish which is important, and is significantly linked to pupil achievement, is praise for school achievements in the language. Of eight aspects of English, Irish, Mathematics and Project work, most parents 'often' praise English reading (73.1%) and Mathematics (72.9%) (data not in tabular form). Only in the case of three aspects of Irish do the percentages of parents 'often' offering praise fall below

Table 10. Percentage of parents (respondent) in ordinary and all-Irish of schools according to the frequency with which they speak Irish to their child.

Parent speaks Irish to child –	Ordinary	All-Irish
Always	0.1% *(0.09)*	1.1% *(0.55)*
Very often	1.0% *(0.24)*	5.2% *(1.04)*
Often	2.2% *(0.29)*	15.6% *(1.97)*
Occasionally	20.6% *(0.82)*	43.4% *(1.73)*
Seldom	33.1% *(0.99)*	25.5% *(1.17)*
Never	42.3% *(1.28)*	8.4% *(1.45)*
Missing	0.7% *(0.15)*	0.8% *(0.45)*

Standard error printed in italics. N Ordinary = 2744, N All-Irish = 609.

Table 11. Percentage of parents in ordinary and all-Irish schools according to the general attitude towards Irish which they try to encourage in their child.

General attitude to Irish encouraged by parent	Ordinary	All-Irish
I let my child know that Irish is important	32.5% *(1.04)*	55.0% *(2.13)*
I leave it up to my child to develop his/her own attitude to Irish	66.2% *(1.02)*	44.3% *(2.09)*
I discourage my child from taking Irish seriously	0.7% *(0.20)*	0.1% *(0.12)*
Missing	0.6% *(0.14)*	0.6% *(0.40)*

Standard error printed in italics. N Ordinary = 2744, N All-Irish = 609.

50%: 49.8% in the case of Irish reading, 48.2% for Irish Writing, and only 38.4% in the case of Spoken/Oral Irish. At the other extreme, while only 2.3% of parents said that they 'hardly ever' praised the English reading achievements of their children, and only 2% hardly ever praised their mathematics achievements, 25% hardly ever praised the child's spoken/oral Irish. Taken together with their responses to other questions reported above, and in Harris et al (2006), it is clear that most parents who have children in ordinary schools adopt a relatively 'hands-off' approach to the learning of Irish.

Can the growth in the all-Irish sector compensate for decline in ordinary schools?

Is it possible that the substantial decline between 1985 and 2002 in achievement in Irish Listening in ordinary schools described earlier might be linked in some way to the dramatic growth in the population of all-Irish schools during the same period? One version of this hypothesis is that the particular pupils who were 'lost' to ordinary schools since 1985, and were 'gained' by all-Irish schools, were likely to have the kind of educational, linguistic or family background that would tend to produce relatively high levels of interest and achievement in Irish anyway.

Data presented earlier, for example, confirm that all-Irish parents tend to speak Irish more often with their children than parents in ordinary schools do. Harris et al 2006 in additional analyses show that in *both* ordinary and all-Irish schools, variations in parental ability and use are associated with significant differences in achievement in Irish.

One test of this hypothesis would be to hypothetically 'relocate' all the all-Irish pupils (with their 'all-Irish' level of achievement) 'back' into ordinary schools. The idea (Harris et al, 2006) is to estimate the effect on the Irish Listening mean raw score in ordinary schools of reintroducing the 'high-Irish-potential' pupils which they had 'lost' to all-Irish schools, reweighting as appropriate to take account of the greater density of sampling which we used in the case of the relatively small all-Irish sector. We assume for the purpose of this test that high-Irish-potential pupils perform comparatively well, achieving a mean raw score of 66 out of 75 on the Irish Listening Test (this is the 1985 mean for all-Irish pupils given in Table 1). We will assume that other pupils (non 'high-Irish-potential' pupils) achieve a mean of 34 out of 75 (this is the mean raw score of pupils in ordinary schools in 2002).

It was found that the effect of this relocation was to raise the overall mean for ordinary schools to only 35.3 (as opposed to the actual mean of 34 achieved in 2002 and the much higher mean of 46.9 achieved in 1985). Incidentally, by assuming that these pupils whom we are 'relocating' in 2002 are performing at the average level for all-Irish schools, we are maximising their potential to 'correct' ordinary school achievement in 2002 back to its 1985 level. In reality, if high-Irish-potential pupils had stayed in ordinary schools, it is extremely unlikely that their Irish achievement would have been as high as we estimated it. The fact that, even with the benefit of this very generous correction, the adjusted mean score for Irish Listening in 2002 still only rises to 35.3 means that we have to look elsewhere for an explanation for the decline in Irish achievement in ordinary schools between 1985 and 2002. It also undermines any notion that all-Irish schools, rapid and all as their growth has been, are presently taking up the slack in language revitalisation and maintenance terms nationally which resulted from the fall-off in achievement in ordinary schools.

Diminished contribution of the primary sector to the revitalisation of Irish

This study of long-term trends in achievement in Irish indicates clearly that the traditional language revitalisation function of primary schools, which had remained reasonably stable during the 1960s to 1980s, has been seriously weakened in the last two decades. The study also provides information on at least some of the key sociolinguistic and educational factors which are plausibly related to this decline.

This new information, added to that available from a number of studies conducted prior to and during the 17-year period under consideration (Harris, 1983, 1984; Harris and Murtagh, 1987, 1988a, 1988b, 1996, 1997, 1999) allows us to construct at least a preliminary account of how this decline came about. One clear message emerging from all this work is that a range of factors, both inside and outside the school, combine to determine the eventual level of pupil achievement in Irish. But there is no sure way to retrospectively identify the precise set of factors which contributed to the decline in achievement in ordinary schools since the 1980s, or the order of importance of these factors. The analysis presented below, therefore, is intended to contribute to a wider discussion on the issues rather than to be a definitive statement of causes and remedies.

Our argument is that a combination of negative and challenging factors affecting pupil achievement in Irish in ordinary schools developed in the late 1980s and through the 1990s. We will group these under three main headings: (1) Front-line issues such as a lack of a suitable method and materials for teaching Irish, the contraction of the core time for Irish, and a decline in teaching through Irish outside the Irish lesson proper; (2) The beginning of some change in the central dynamic which has always driven the revitalisation function of primary schools i.e. the willingness of teachers to draw on their own reservoir of positive attitudes and commitment, as it were, in transmitting the language to children on behalf of society; and (3) A weakening in the broader support and policy context for the revitalisation function of schools, linked in part to major structural changes in education inside and outside the Department of Education and Science (DES) which occurred during the period under consideration. Each of these issues will now be examined in turn.

Frontline causative factors: Materials, core time and Irish-medium instruction

Central to the decline in achievement is the fact that the audio-visual curriculum and associated teaching materials (the *Nuachúrsaí*) used in the vast majority of schools in the period under consideration were unsuitable. Despite increasing dissatisfaction among teachers going back to the mid-1980s, these were not finally replaced until the revised curriculum, *Curaclam na Bunscoile* (NCCA, 1999 a,b,c) was published. Dissatisfaction with the *Nuachúrsaí* had focussed on at least three issues over time: the difficulty level of the materials, the dated and unsuitable content of the lessons themselves, and the structural-linguistic/audio-visual teaching approach involved.

All three of these criticisms have been supported by research findings (Harris, 1984,1996; Harris et al 1996; Harris and Murtagh, 1999). The strong evidence that a variety of other factors, a number of them discussed below, also contribute significantly to pupil achievement, however, makes it extremely unlikely that the change in methods and materials which have now taken place will be sufficient to solve the problem (Harris, 1983; Harris and Murtagh, 1987, 1988a, 1988b, 1999).

A second causative factor must certainly be the contraction in core time. Three separate national surveys between 1976 and 1985 showed that the amount of time per week spent on Irish varied from 5.6 to 5.1 hours. In the introduction to *Curaclam na Bunscoile* (NCCA, 1999c), however, the core ('minimum') time for Irish as a second language is specified as 3.5 hours. While there was some newspaper comment at the time to the effect that this represented a reduction in the amount of time for Irish, there seemed to be a general acceptance that time pressure in the curriculum for a number of years previously had already probably reduced the real time for Irish to something like that level. The contraction in core time for Irish is very likely to have contributed to the fall in standards documented here. As Johnstone (2002: 20) points out, "in all countries ´time´ is an important factor, but in some it is vitally important where there is very little exposure to the target language in society...".

The reduction in core time was a greater loss for Irish than was the corresponding reduction in core time for other subjects. This is because the use of Irish does not easily extend beyond the Irish slot without the special effort of the teacher. English reading, writing, and mathematics, for example, extend easily, naturally and by necessity into other areas of the curriculum all the time, without any specific action by the teacher. In many ordinary schools, the reduction in core time for Irish will have seriously undermined the only foothold the language had in the curriculum.

The third front line factor is the reduction in the informal 'extended' programme. Data from a number of studies show that teaching through Irish (outside the Irish lesson proper) is a very powerful factor determining achievement in the language (Harris, 1983; 1984; Harris and Murtagh, 1988; Harris et al 2006).

While only a minority of schools and classes may adopt this approach, that minority within the mainstream population of ordinary schools accounts for a very great absolute number of pupils. If this kind of Irish-medium teaching had increased during the 1985–2002 period it could have gone a considerable way to compensating for the effects of the decline in core time for Irish just described. It is clear from DES statistics (Department of Education and Science, 1986; 2002), however, that what in reality has happened is the opposite — teaching through Irish declined significantly between 1985 and 2002.

Teachers and schools as agents of revitalisation: The beginnings of change

Before examining the issues of changing teacher attitudes, some mention should be made of the unique role which schools and teachers play in relation to Irish compared to other subjects. Through no fault of schools or teachers, Irish tends to be relatively 'sealed off' within ordinary schools compared to other subjects. Pupils have little or no interactive contact with the spoken language outside school. This makes it difficult for both teachers and pupils to identify an immediate goal or motivation outside school for learning to speak the language in the classroom. Even within schools, it is very easy for Irish to become sealed off within the Irish slot in ways that other subjects, such as English reading or mathematics, do not.

Another aspect of this isolation of schools concerns parents. We have already presented data on the hands-off attitude of parents to Irish. It is a subject which is left largely to the school. The great majority seldom or never speak Irish to their child, tend to praise achievements in Irish (particularly spoken Irish) much less often than they praise other subjects, and leave it up to the children to develop their own attitude to Irish. It is not that these same parents are unconcerned about their children's progress or that the wider Irish public are not concerned about the language. Data in Harris et al (2006) show that parents are as keen as they have ever been that their children would learn Irish and, in the majority of cases, believe the school is doing everything possible to ensure that that is achieved. It is just that for personal and historical reasons many parents are not engaged with Irish, or with their children's learning it, in the same way as they are engaged with other subjects.

One of the consequences of this is that Irish depends on the attitudes, efforts, and commitment of individual schools and teachers in a way that other subjects do not. It is difficult to imagine teachers having personal attitudes to subjects such as mathematics or English that would be related to their day-to-day work in these subject areas in the way their attitude to Irish would be related.

Data in Harris et al 2006 show that of eight factors which might determine the strength of teachers' emphasis on Irish, it was their own attitudes which they rated as most important in determining the emphasis they place on and the time they devoted to Irish. In one limited sense, this state of affairs — the centrality of teacher attitudes and contribution — has been very much to the advantage of Irish in the past. This is because, as shown earlier, teachers have more positive attitudes to Irish than parents and the general population. This confirms data elsewhere (CLAR 1975; INTO 1985a,b; Ó Riagáin, 1986: 13).

But the other side of this coin is that because the emphasis on Irish in school depends so much on the drive and commitment of individual teachers, the consequences can be very great indeed if teachers' attitudes, motivation, self-esteem, or professional satisfaction in teaching Irish decline. Leaving aside for a moment the causes, our results here show that teacher attitudes have begun to change since the mid-1980s. There was a significant decrease between 1985 and 2002, from 80.3% to 55.4%, in the percentage of pupils whose teachers derived satisfaction from teaching Irish. Other data (Harris et al 2006) also show significant declines in the percentage whose attitude to Irish being taught in primary school was favourable, and in the percentage who felt that less time should be spent on Irish. Most important of all perhaps, the key teacher attitude mentioned above has also begun to change. There has been a significant decline in the percentage of teachers who say that the amount of time and emphasis they devote to Irish is determined, above all, by their *own outlook and opinion*. In other words, the reservoir of positive attitudes and motivation which teachers possess is no longer being harnessed, as it were, on behalf of the language at primary level in the same way it was in the mid 1980s. This would be more serious, of course, if it should represent the beginning of a trend.

One factor which may have contributed to changing teacher attitudes, ironically enough, is the growth of all-Irish schools. When all-Irish numbers were very small in the early 1980s, their success could not really overshadow the achievements of ordinary schools. But with their growth and more visible presence around the country in recent years, teachers in ordinary schools may sometimes have felt that a certain kind of leadership in relation to Irish had passed to these new schools. In most ordinary schools, where the emphasis on Irish depends on the commitment and interest of the individual teacher, issues of professional esteem and satisfaction such as these are probably more important than they are in the case of other school subjects.

A central aspect of the reward of the job must be the teacher's perception that he or she is operating in a context, and with the kinds of supports, which allow a worthwhile level of pupil proficiency in Irish to be achieved. The growth of all-Irish schools may have redefined some of these perceptions.

Planning and support: Institutional responsiveness and changing structures

Because of the isolation of schools and teachers in relation to Irish, responsibility for the rapid identification of emerging system-wide problems, and for the formulation of an adequate response to them, rests more heavily on official institutions in the case of Irish than it would in the case of other school subjects. We have already mentioned the most obvious problem of official responsiveness during the period 1985–2002 — the delay in providing a new curriculum and materials for Irish. But another problematic aspect of it is that the scope of the response has often been too narrowly defined. Ideally, it should cover the full set of educational and language planning issues relevant to the decline in pupil achievement — the time pressure on Irish, the decline in teaching through Irish, the relative lack of parental engagement with Irish in school, the deterioration in teacher satisfaction in teaching Irish, and even the lack of support for Irish outside the school.

A related issue from a language planning point of view is the likelihood that the deficiencies in official responsiveness — and ultimately the decline in the effectiveness of primary schools as revitalisation agents — are connected to major changes in educational administration nationally which took place in the 1980s and 1990s. In 1985, both the Irish curriculum and the new Irish conversation courses which were then introduced had been developed by the inspectorate under the auspices of the DES. It was the National Council for Curriculum and Assessment, however, which developed the present curriculum published in 1999. New Irish courses for ordinary schools were then produced by the commercial publishers, and a new statutory body, an *Chomhairle Um Oideachas Gaeltachta agus Gaelscolaíochta*, was assigned a range of important new functions in relation to Irish in education including the provision of materials in Irish for all-Irish and Gaeltacht schools. During this same period, the school inspectorate was radically reorganised as part of a major restructuring and re-examination of roles within the DES which had originated in the Strategic Management Initiative (Delivering Better Government: Strategic Management Initiative, 1996; Department of Education and Science, 2000).

Without in any way questioning the general merits of these structural and institutional changes, it is worthwhile considering whether in every respect they were positive for Irish.

As long as Irish was installed in the key decision-making environment of the DES, the language was guaranteed a high priority and enjoyed relatively little curricular competition. In addition, emerging problems could be detected early, decisions on a response could be taken quickly and the connections between the educational and language-maintenance aspects of problems were transparent. The location of these functions in the DES also provided a more visible official commitment and leadership in relation to the language, communicating in a direct way where ownership of, and responsibility for, the various problems and issues ultimately lay.

A long-term exercise in educational and language planning

An adequate response to the problems of declining pupil achievement levels and growing disenchantment among teachers can be built on the analysis just presented. The central issue is to acknowledge the complexity of the problem and to enlarge our existing definition of it.

The second major requirement is to develop an adequate plan of action which is equal to the range of difficulties identified in the present study and in previous research. Ideally, this plan should cover not just Irish as a subject but the wider use of Irish in school and the supports available in the home and in the community. This exercise would involve research, development and creative work designed to provide solutions to the challenges presented by the real sociolinguistic situation in which schools operate. It would need to take account both of the educational aspects of the issue and the national aim of promoting bilingualism and the wider use of Irish. A language planning exercise of the kind proposed would be much more effective if explicit political agreement at a national level was secured in advance for its goals and implementation processes.

References

CLAR (Committee on Irish Language Attitudes Research). 1975. *Report*. Dublin: Stationery Office.

Delivering Better Government: Strategic Management Initiative. 1996. *Second Report to Government of the Co-ordinating Group of Secretaries: A Programme of Change for the Irish Civil Service*. Dublin: Government Publications.

Department of Education. 1978. *Lá faoin tuath / Sean Neidí. Cúrsaí Comhrá Gaeilge le haghaidh ranganna sinsearacha.* Dublin: Stationery Office.

Department of Education. 1986. *Tuarascáil staitistiúil (Statistical report) 1985/1986.* Dublin: Stationery Office.

Department of Education and Science. 2000. *Review of Department's Operations, Systems and Staffing Needs* (Cromien Report). Retrieved June 2005. http://www.education.ie/servlet/ blobservlet/des_cromien_report.pdf

Department of Education and Science. 2002. *Tuarascáil staitistiúil (Statistical report) 2001/2002.* Dublin: Stationery Office.

Dorian, N. 1988. The Celtic languages in the British Isles. In *International Handbook of Bilingualism and Bilingual Education,* C.B. Paulston (ed.), 109–140. Westport: Greeenwood Press.

Fishman, J. 1991. *Reversing Language Shift: Theoretical and Empirical Foundations of Assistance to Threatened Languages.* Clevedon: Multilingual Matters.

Fishman, J. (ed.). 2001. *Can Threatened Languages be Saved?* Clevedon: Multilingual Matters.

Fontes, P. & Kellaghan, T. 1977. *The New Primary School Curriculum: Its Implementation and Effects.* Dublin: Educational Research Centre.

Harris, J. 1982. Achievement in spoken Irish at the end of primary school. *Irish Journal of Education* 16: 85–116.

Harris, J. 1983. Relationships between achievement in spoken Irish and demographic, administrative and teaching factors. *Irish Journal of Education* 17: 5–34.

Harris, J. 1984. *Spoken Irish in Primary Schools.* Dublin: Institiúid Teangeolaíochta Éireann.

Harris, J. 1988. Spoken Irish in the primary school system. *International Journal of the Sociology of Language* 70: 69–87.

Harris, J. 1997. Speaking proficiency in Irish in primary school children: Educational and sociolinguistic factors. In *Plurilingual XVIII: Recent Studies in Contact Llinguistics,* W. Wolck & A.De Houwer (eds), 129–135. Bonn: Dummler.

Harris, J. & Murtagh, L. 1987. Irish and English in Gaeltacht primary schools. In *Third International Conference on Minority Languages: Celtic Papers,* G. Mac Eoin, A. Ahlqvist & D.Ó hAodha (eds), 104–124. Clevedon: Multilingual Matters.

Harris, J. & Murtagh L. 1988a. Ability and Communication in Learning Irish. Ms, Institiúid Teangeolaíochta Éireann, Dublin.

Harris, J. & Murtagh L. 1988b. National assessment of Irish-language speaking and listening skills in primary-school children: Research issues in the evaluation of school-based heritage-language programmes. *Language, Culture and Curriculum* 1(2): 85–130.

Harris, J. & Murtagh, L. 1996. Topic and language activity in teaching Irish at sixth grade in primary school: A classroom observation study. In *Language, Education and Society in a Changing World,* T. Hickey & J. Williams (eds), 209–220. Clevedon: Multilingual Matters.

Harris, J. & Murtagh, L. 1997. Speech and silence in the Irish language class. In *Dán do oide,* A. Ahlqvist & V. Capkova (eds), 221–241. Dublin: Institiúid Teangeolaíochta Éireann.

Harris, J. & Murtagh, L. 1999. *Teaching and Learning Irish in Primary Schools.* Dublin: Institiúid Teangeolaíochta Éireann.

Harris, J., Forde, P., Archer, P., Nic Fhearaile, S. & O Gorman, M. 2006. *Irish in Primary School: Long-term National Trends in Achievement.* Dublin: Irish Government Department of Education and Science.

Harris, J., Ó Néill, P., Uí Dhufaigh, M. & O Súilleabháin, E. 1996. *Cúrsaí nua Gaeilge na bunscoile: Moltaí agus ábhar samplach. Imleabhar 1: Naíonáin Shóisearacha — Rang 2.* Dublin: Institiúid Teangeolaíochta Éireann.

INTO (Irish National Teachers' Organisation): Education Committee. 1976. *Primary School Curriculum: Curriculum Questionnaire Analysis*. Dublin: Author.

INTO. 1985a. *The Irish Language in Primary Education: Summary of INTO Survey of Teachers' Attitudes to the Position of Irish in Primary Education*. Dublin: Author.

INTO. 1985b. *The Irish Language in Primary Schools: Summary of the Main Findings of a Survey of Public Attitudes by the Market Research Bureau of Ireland*. Dublin: Author.

Johnstone, R. 2002. *Addressing 'the Age Factor': Some Implications for Language Policy*. (Guide for the development of Language Education Policies in Europe: From Linguistic Diversity to Plurilingual Education. Reference study). Strasbourg: Council of Europe.

Macnamara, J. 1966. *Bilingualism and primary education. A study of Irish experience*. Edinburgh: University Press.

Macnamara, J. 1971. Successes and failures in the movement for the restoration of Irish. In *Can Language be Planned?*, J. Rubin & B.H. Jernudd (eds), 65–94. Honolulu HI: The University Press of Hawaii,

NCCA (National Council for Curriculum and Assessment). 1999a. *Curaclam na bunscoile: Gaeilge: Teanga*. Dublin: Stationery Office.

NCCA. 1999b. *Curaclam na bunscoile: Gaeilge: Teanga: Treoirlínte do Mhúinteoirí*. Dublin: Stationery Office.

NCCA. 1999c. *Curaclam na bunscoile: Réamhrá. Primary school curriculum: Introduction*. Dublin: Stationery Office.

Ó Buachalla, S. 1984. Educational policy and the role of the Irish language from 1831 to 1981. *European Journal of Education* 19(1): 75–92.

Ó Buachalla, S. 1988. *Educational Policy in Twentieth Century Ireland*. Dublin: Wolfhound Press.

Ó Domhnalláin, T. 1987. *The Irish Language in Primary Education: Republic of Ireland*. Ljouwert: Fryske Akademy.

Ó Domhnalláin, T. & Ó Gliasáin, M. 1976. *Audio-Visual Methods v. a.b.c Methods in the Teaching of Irish*. Dublin: Institiúid Teangeolaíochta Éireann.

Ó Riagáin, P. 1986. *Public and Teacher Attitudes towards Irish in the Schools. A Review of Recent Studies* [Occasional Paper 6]. Dublin: Institiúid Teangeolaíochta Éireann.

Ó Riagáin, P. 1997. *Language Policy and Social Reproduction: Ireland 1893–1993*. Oxford: Clarendon Press.

Ó Riagáin, P. 2001. Irish language production and reproduction 1981–1996. In *Can Threatened Languages be Saved?*, J. Fishman (ed.), pp. 195–214. Clevedon: Multilingual Matters.

Spolsky, B. 2004. *Language Policy*. Cambridge: CUP.

Wright, S. 2004. *Language Policy and Language Planning: From Nationalism to Globalisation*. Basingstroke: Palgrave Macmillan.

Author's address

John Harris
Trinity College Dublin
Dublin 2
Ireland

harrisjo@tcd.ie

Current challenges in bilingual education in Wales

W. Gwyn Lewis
Prifysgol Bangor University

In Wales, bilingual education in Welsh and English has an increasingly high profile and Wales shares international leadership of bilingual education policies and practices alongside other countries where bilingual education flourishes. Ever since the first designated Welsh-medium primary school was opened in 1939, Welsh-medium and bilingual education has spread across Wales.

This poses both an opportunity and a challenge to educators, since classes may well contain a wide linguistic variety of native speakers and learners of Welsh. This also gives rise to variations in teaching methodologies and in the allocation of languages across the curriculum, with growing experimentation in the concurrent use of both languages within the same lesson period.

New research seeks to develop a profile of language allocation in bilingual schools in Wales, and to construct a typology of bilingual education that is empirical as well as conceptual. It also seeks to critique current typologies of bilingual education.

This paper will commence with a brief overview of the development of the Welsh language and its role within the bilingual education system in Wales (including current statistics), before going on to discuss the research work in progress and present some early emerging issues and challenges.

Introduction

Wales, with a population of close to 3 million, is located on the western shores of the United Kingdom and is a relatively small country of about 20,779 km². It is about 275 km from north to south and some 160 km across its widest point from east to west. To the east, Wales borders England and the west coast borders the Irish Sea, with the Bristol Channel separating the south of Wales from the south of England.

Alongside Scotland and England, Wales "is one of the three constituent nations that comprise the current multilingual national British state ... Moreover, unlike Scotland ... Wales has had a much longer and more assimilative relationship with

AILA Review 21 (2008), 69–86. DOI 10.1075/aila.21.06lew
ISSN 1461–0213 / E-ISSN 1570–5595 © John Benjamins Publishing Company

England" (May 2000:103) which, consequently, has contributed to the lack of status for the Welsh language in Wales over the centuries.

The Welsh Language

Welsh — like its sister languages Breton, Cornish, Irish, Scots Gaelic and Manx — evolved from the Celtic branch of what linguists term *Indo-European*, and of the languages now spoken in Britain, Welsh has by far the oldest roots, going back at least 2,500 years and perhaps 4,000 years, compared with little more than 1,500 years in the cases of English and Scots Gaelic (Davies 1993:12). Welsh also boasts a rich cultural and literary tradition, dating back to early heroic verse in Old Welsh in the sixth century.

Welsh and English have co-existed in Wales for over six centuries, ever since the "colonisation of Wales by England in the fourteenth and fifteenth centuries [which] led to the area's increasing anglicisation" (May 2000:103) resulting in Welsh becoming a minority language within the country in terms of power and status.

However, there are over half a million Welsh speakers in Wales today and Figure 1 below illustrates their distribution and concentration across the country. The most western areas — which have more than 48% of the population able to speak Welsh — constitute what is often referred to as the 'Welsh-speaking heartland' and the further east one moves there is a tendency for the number and prevalence of Welsh speakers to decrease.

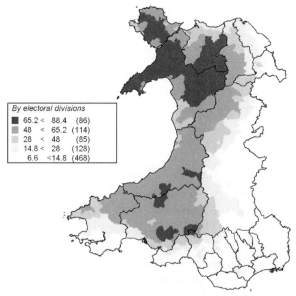

By electoral divisions
65.2 < 88.4   (86)
48   < 65.2 (114)
28   < 48   (85)
14.8 < 28   (128)
6.6   <14.8 (468)

Figure 1. Percentage able to speak Welsh, 2001: all aged 3 and over (source: Hywel M. Jones, Welsh Language Board)

At the beginning of the twentieth century, however, the Welsh language was spoken by around half the population of Wales. The 1911 Census recorded that nearly a million people regarded themselves as Welsh speakers. However, since that Census, the number of Welsh speakers decreased steadily until fairly recently and many different reasons are cited for this (http://bwrdd-yr-iaith.org.uk), for example:

- migration patterns from rural to urban areas (and to England and abroad) in search of work;
- the effect of tourism and inward migration of English speakers to traditionally Welsh-speaking areas;
- the demise of rural communities;
- the heartland areas often associated with relatively less employment/economic strengths;
- increased availability of English-language news and entertainment media, together with the effect of mass communication (e.g. telephone, the internet, e-mail, text-messaging);
- a general secularisation of society, leading to a decline in chapel and church attendance, on which so many traditional Welsh-medium activities were centered;
- industrialization;
- transport and communication (e.g. motorways, rail, air travel);
- anglicization of education.

The combined influence of these factors, among others, led to the erosion of the language in many communities which were once almost entirely Welsh-speaking. However, the latest Census figures of 2001 show that — unlike the majority of the world's other small languages which are dying rapidly — the number of people speaking Welsh today is increasing, see Figure 2.

Of all aged 3 and over, 20.8% (582,368) of the population can speak at least some Welsh, 16.3% (457,946) can understand, speak, read and write Welsh (i.e. have the full range of skills), and 4.9% (138,416) can understand spoken Welsh only (National

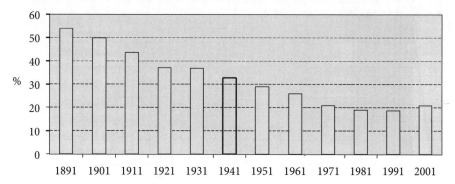

Figure 2. 1891–2001 Census results: % able to speak Welsh (source: Hywel M. Jones, Welsh Language Board)

Assembly for Wales 2003). This inter-generational transmission, together with bilingual education, is reproducing the language in the young people of Wales — against
the trend in minority languages in the world.

Significantly, the highest percentages of Welsh speakers in 2001 were found amongst
children (40.8% in children 5–15 years). Indeed, the percentage of Welsh speakers in the
younger 5–9 and 10–14 age groups has been higher than the percentage in the 15–24 age
groups since 1971, and the difference between the percentages of those groups has been
increasing every decade since 1971, as can be seen from Figures 3 and 4.

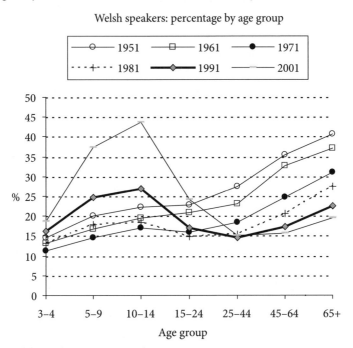

Figure 3. Welsh speakers, percentage by age group
Source: *Census 2001: Main Statistics About Welsh,* issued on the Welsh Language Board's website on 23
September 2003 (http://www.byig-wlb.org.uk)

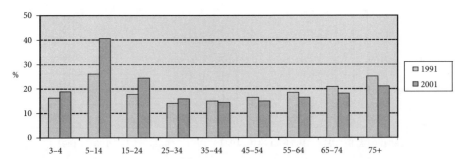

Figure 4. Census results: % able to speak Welsh by age (source: Hywel M. Jones, Welsh
Language Board)

As can be seen from the statistics, the largest increase in Welsh speakers was among the youngest age groups in 2001. This probably reflects the increase in Welsh-medium education across Wales and the effect of the 1988 Education Reform Act and the introduction of the National Curriculum. Such policy changes resulted in the Welsh language being taught either as a first or second language to almost every pupil in Wales up to, and including, key stage 4 (14–16 year olds): 98.1 % of pupils in maintained primary schools and 99.1% of pupils in Years 7–11 in 2006–2007 (Welsh Assembly Government 2007a).

The Welsh language in education in Wales: a brief history

In twenty first century Wales, bilingual education (i.e. Welsh and English) has an increasingly high profile and — alongside other countries where bilingual education flourishes — Wales shares international leadership of bilingual education philosophy, policies and practices. The last sixty years have seen a rapid growth in the development of Welsh-medium and bilingual education across Wales, with the education system being regarded as playing a vital role in ensuring the inter-generational transmission of the Welsh language and being labelled "a major plank in language revitalisation and language reversal" (Baker 2004: 1). It can be said that the education system — as in many other minority language situations — has become the basis of reversing language shift with respect to the Welsh language in Wales.

With the exception of the network of Sunday schools developed by the Welsh Non-Conformist movement in the eighteenth century — which resulted in the Welsh becoming a literate nation long before the establishment of a national education system — the language of formal education in Wales up to the late nineteenth century was predominantly English. The passage of the 'Act of Union' through English parliament in 1536, incorporating Wales into England, deemed that no person should hold public office if he could not speak English. Inevitably, this was to have a detrimental effect on the use of Welsh in education. Not until the late nineteenth century did the language receive any recognition in the field of formal education. The infamous report of the Committee of Enquiry into the role of education in Wales — published in 1847 and referred to as *Brad y Llyfrau Gleision* ('The Treachery of the Blue Books') — insisted that the moral and material condition of Wales could only be improved by the introduction of English, arguing that "the Welsh language is a vast drawback to Wales, and a manifold barrier to the moral progress and commercial prosperity of the people. It is not easy to over-estimate its evil effects" (Roberts 1998: 204). This, together with the controversial 'Welsh Not' (a piece of wood hung around the necks of children heard speaking Welsh in some schools, leading to corporal punishment at the end of the day) and the Education Act of 1870, which established a complete network of English-medium schools, contributed to the exclusion of Welsh within the formal education system (Davies 1993: 13–67; May 2000: 104).

However, at the end of the nineteenth century, the work of the Society for the Utilization of Welsh in Education, established in 1885 — together with the recommendations of the Royal Commission on Elementary Education in 1890 — paved the way for grants being made to schools which taught Welsh and authorized the use of bilingual books in schools. The significance of this concession has been summarized by Davies (1993: 50) as "It was ... a development of fundamental importance that Welsh had won a toehold in the education system; indeed, all the advances made by Welsh in schools in the twentieth century had their origins in the victory of 1890."

The twentieth century saw more significant developments: the appointment of O.M. Edwards as Chief Inspector for Wales of the new Board of Education in 1907 who played a crucial role in promoting positive attitudes towards the Welsh language in schools, and the publication of the Board's report, *Welsh in Education and Life*, in 1927 which inquired into the position occupied by Welsh in the educational system in Wales and advised how its study may be promoted. For more information on the history of Welsh in education, see Davies (1993), Williams (2002, 2003), and Jones and Martin-Jones (2004).

The first *Ysgol Gymraeg* (Welsh-medium school) was opened in Aberystwyth in 1939 by Sir Ifan ab Owen Edwards (O.M. Edwards' son) as an independent designated Welsh-medium primary school with seven pupils, established by a group of enthusiastic Welsh-speaking parents under the auspices of *Urdd Gobaith Cymru* (Williams 2002, 2003). Since 1939, Welsh-medium and bilingual primary education has developed and flourished across Wales, with an increasing number of pupils from non-Welsh-speaking homes taking advantage of this provision through the medium of Welsh. However, by 1939, many primary schools in rural areas were using Welsh as their natural medium of instruction, thanks to the efforts and influence of Sir Ifan ab Owen Edwards' father, O. M. Edwards, in his role as Chief Inspector for Wales. The establishment of a Welsh-medium school in an Anglicised town or industrial region was a revolutionary concept in 1939 (Williams 2003: 10).

The Education Act of 1944 in England and Wales stated that pupils were to be educated in accordance with the wishes of their parents (Section 76). The act allowed Local Education Authorities in Wales to consider opening Welsh-medium schools, and as a result of parental pressure, the first Welsh-medium state-funded primary school run by a Local Education Authority was opened in Llanelli in south-west Wales on St. David's Day 1947 (Williams, 2002, 2003) and the first Welsh-medium secondary school, Ysgol Glan Clwyd, in the old Flintshire in September 1956 (Williams, 2002, 2003). Initially, these Welsh-medium schools catered for children for whom Welsh was their first language, and therefore could be classified as *heritage or maintenance language education* or *community language education* (Baker 1993a: 162; Johnstone 2002). However, since the 1960s, 1970s, and 1980s, there has been a dramatic increase in the numbers of non-Welsh-speaking parents choosing Welsh-medium education for their children — which, for them, can be classified as *immersion education* (Baker 1993a: 229; Johnstone 2002). The Welsh Assembly Government (2003) also acknowledges that education through the medium of Welsh has increased steadily in recent years and emphasises the essential role of education through the medium of Welsh to develop strong bilingual skills among pupils.

Welsh in schools

The current statistical analysis by the Welsh Assembly Government (2007a), *Welsh in Schools 2007*, points to the fact that Welsh-medium education is well-embedded in the Welsh education system (Table 1).

Welsh-medium primary and secondary education in the twenty first century embraces pupils from a wide and diverse linguistic spectrum. Whereas the first Welsh-medium schools (or *ysgolion Cymraeg*) were established with the main aim of providing Welsh-speaking pupils with education in their first language, by today in areas such as north-east Wales and south-east Wales, the majority of children come from non-Welsh-speaking homes. Only 0.2% of primary school pupils (and 0.0% of secondary school pupils) in the south-east county of Newport speak Welsh at home (Welsh Assembly Government, 2007a, Table 4 and Table 17). Across Wales, the pattern varies as can be seen from the following statistics in Table 2.

Consequently, classes in primary and secondary schools can easily contain a wide linguistic variety: pupils who are fluent in Welsh, pupils with a little knowledge of the language, children from completely non-Welsh-speaking homes, as well as recent

Table 1. Statistical analysis by the Welsh Assembly Government (2007a: 3)

Primary schools at January 2007
- There were 466 Welsh speaking primary schools (30.5 per cent of the total number) at January 2007 with 54,100 pupils on roll, eight more schools and 1,200 more pupils than in 2006.
- The percentage of primary school pupils taught in classes where Welsh is used as the main medium of teaching rose from 20.1 per cent in 2006 to 20.3 per cent in 2007.
- The percentage of pupils assessed in Welsh at the end of Key Stage 1 increased slightly from 20.0 per cent in 2006 to 20.3 per cent in 2007.
- The percentage of pupils assessed in Welsh at the end of Key Stage 2 increased slightly from 19.3 per cent in 2006 to 19.5 per cent in 2007.

Secondary schools at January 2007
- 15.4 per cent of pupils in year groups 7–11 (compulsory school age) in maintained secondary schools were taught Welsh as a first language, up from 15.2 per cent in 2006. A further 83.7 per cent were taught Welsh as a second language.
- The percentage of Year 7 pupils taught Welsh first language decreased slightly from 16.7 per cent in 2006 to 16.2 per cent in 2007.
- The percentage of pupils assessed in Welsh first language at the end of Key Stage 3 decreased from 15.7 per cent in 2006 to 15.3 per cent in 2007, slightly higher than the percentage of Year 9 pupils reported as having studied Welsh as a first language (15.2 per cent).

Table 2. Variation in the pattern across Wales of Maintained primary and secondary school pupils who speak Welsh at home (Source: Welsh Assembly Government, 2007a, Tables 4 and 15)

	Primary		Secondary	
	No.	%	No.	%
Isle of Anglesey	1,448	33.5	1,511	39.5
Gwynedd	4,092	52.7	4,266	59.2
Conwy	773	11.0	701	10.8
Denbighshire	562	8.7	779	11.4
Flintshire	214	2.0	184	2.0
Wrexham	237	2.7	241	3.6
Powys	592	6.8	499	6.3
Ceredigion	1,280	30.9	1,565	37.7
Pembrokeshire	463	5.7	551	7.7
Carmarthenshire	2,491	21.4	2,487	23.1
Swansea	304	2.0	434	3.3
Neath Port Talbot	473	5.1	553	6.3
Bridgend	186	1.9	13	0.2
The Vale of Glamorgan	371	4.0	378	4.6
Rhondda, Cynon, Taff	770	4.8	696	4.5
Merthyr Tydfil	60	1.5	5	0.1
Caerphilly	47	0.4	56	0.5
Blaenau Gwent	35	0.7	1	0.0
Torfaen	17	0.3	62	0.9
Monmouthshire	56	1.0	5	0.1
Newport	23	0.2	4	0.0
Cardiff	838	3.9	677	3.7
Wales	15,332	7.6	15,668	8.6

newcomers to Wales (from inside or outside the United Kingdom) who have no prior knowledge of the language — but wish to acquire it through the education system. In schools across Wales, the ratio between pupils from Welsh-speaking homes and those from non-Welsh-speaking homes varies considerably and this has far-reaching implications as regards balance between Welsh L1 and L2 pupils in a school, differentiated teaching methods in respect of L1 maintenance and L2 immersion, grouping of pupils (Baker and Jones 1998:508–17) and, consequently, teacher training (Lewis 2006:21–35). Also, in areas which constitute the stronghold of the Welsh language in Wales (mainly the western counties which include a large population of fully fluent bilingual speakers) — where children coming from both Welsh-speaking and English-speaking homes acquire Welsh — there are a variety of factors that influence the acquisition of Welsh in bilinguals, as detailed by Gathercole and Thomas (2005).

That so many non-Welsh-speaking parents choose Welsh-medium (or immersion) education for their children points to the probability that they appreciate the advantages of an immersion education programme — that their children are able to understand, speak, read, write, and use Welsh as proficient as those children coming from Welsh-speaking homes. In addition — and at no cost — they can also understand, speak, read, write and use Welsh in a way that non-Welsh-speaking pupils who follow a traditional programme of Welsh as a second language in an English-medium school cannot normally do. (The National Assembly for Wales' 'government' definition of a Welsh-medium school is one where more than half the subjects of the National Curriculum are taught through the medium of Welsh; in schools which are not defined as Welsh-medium schools, Welsh is taught only as a second language.)

The figures of the Welsh Assembly Government (2007a) show how the percentage of primary school pupils speaking Welsh has risen from 24.6% in 1987 to 36.5% in 2007. Within this 36.5%, it is reported that 12.6% can speak Welsh fluently: 7.6% from Welsh-speaking homes and 5.0% from non-Welsh-speaking homes. The rest (23.9%) can speak Welsh — but not fluently.

For 7.6% of the pupil population in Welsh primary schools, Welsh-medium education is synonymous with heritage or maintenance language education or community language education. For almost every child in the anglicized areas of south-east Wales, Welsh-medium education is immersion education; in the more traditionally Welsh-speaking areas, it is a mixture of maintenance language education and immersion education. Redknap (2006:5) emphasises that Welsh-medium education is characterized by the provision in the same classroom of immersion education and the provision for those who speak Welsh at home.

This is an opportunity and a challenge that faces the system and its development today (Lewis 2006, 2007). Hickey (2001: 444) made similar observations in respect of Irish-medium education in Ireland.

It is significant that *The Annual Report of Her Majesty's Inspector of Education and Training in Wales 2004–2005* (Estyn 2006: 46) refers specifically to the fact that Welsh-medium schools take in a wide range of pupils from diverse backgrounds, suggesting that teachers, consequently, face challenges in modifying their teaching methods in such situations. In particular in schools in the traditionally Welsh-speaking areas of North Wales and West Wales, there are more pupils from non-Welsh-speaking homes. Many teachers in those schools are finding it hard to change their teaching methods to meet the needs of these new groups of pupils.

Whilst there are advantages for L2 pupils from non-Welsh-speaking homes to have access to their fellow L1 pupils as well as to their teacher as models of the Welsh language, it can also be problematic in that the teacher has to cope within the same class with L2 learners who may be at very different levels of proficiency in the target language. In order to do justice to both cohorts of pupils within the system, special attention needs to be paid to the different teaching and learning approaches used in these various contexts.

Defining Welsh-medium or bilingual education

Although Welsh-medium schools were established to give children from Welsh-speaking homes an education through the medium of Welsh, they have always developed the English language skills of all their pupils, and therefore can justifiably be called 'bilingual schools'. This has lead the Welsh Assembly Government to discuss more fully how we define such schools. The definition of a Welsh-speaking school, given by Section 105(7) of the 2002 Education Act, is, in many ways, a simplistic definition because it states that "... a school is Welsh-speaking if more than one half of the following subjects are taught (wholly or partly) in Welsh (a) religious education, and (b) the subjects other than English and Welsh which are foundation subjects in relation to pupils at the school" (http://wales.gov.uk/publications/accessinfo/drnewhomepage/educationdrs2/educationdrs2007/2007549/?lang=en).

The Welsh Assembly Government acknowledges that this definition does not reflect the complexity of the current situation. It points to a reality which is much more complex. The nature of Welsh-medium provision in schools varies between and within authorities. While Welsh is used as the sole medium of teaching for all or most subjects in certain Welsh-medium schools, others provide lessons and/or subjects in a mix of English and Welsh or have separate English-medium and Welsh-medium streams. The example is given of a secondary school which may be categorised as Welsh-speaking if the requisite number of subjects is taught through the medium of Welsh, even if only a small proportion of the pupils on roll actually study through the medium of Welsh.

Redknap (2006: 10–11) reinforces this sentiment by pointing to the uncertainty and ambiguity over the years caused by the lack of clarity concerning the meaning of such terms as 'Welsh-medium', and 'bilingual'. According to her it is not always easy to understand what proportion of a pupil's curricular time is assigned to Welsh and English, which language is the medium of assessment, and which language is used for day-to-day communication at the school. The definition of the Education Act does not give a precise description of the extent of the Welsh-medium teaching in a school, nor does it really reflect the means by which immersion education works.

In practical terms, in the majority of Welsh-medium primary schools, the children are almost totally immersed in Welsh for the first 2–3 years of schooling with English being gradually introduced both as a subject and a medium of teaching in the junior section (ages 7–11) to reach a 50%/50% or 60%/40% balance between Welsh and English by the last year in the primary school. How that sliding-scale is achieved is of paramount interest to us in the research currently undertaken, as there is almost no documentation, formal policy or rationale available.

That Welsh-medium or bilingual provision varies from one Local Education Authority to the next, with schools operating different policies and practices, reflects the *ad-hoc* way in which the sector has developed without any apparent central planning or co-ordination by the State until very recently (Welsh Language Board 2002). It must also be appreciated that the bilingual provision in the most Welsh-speaking areas is different from Welsh-medium provision in the more anglicized areas. Consequently, different Local Education Authorities (LEA) use a variety of definitions to describe their Welsh-medium provision, which can be quite confusing. Schools and LEAs use labels such as 'Welsh-medium', 'bilingual', 'traditional Welsh' and 'natural Welsh' to describe their provision. Sometimes parents find it difficult to fully understand the extent to which individual schools teach through the medium of Welsh or English, or the extent to which they as parents have a choice about language medium for individual pupils in a school. For the Assembly Government it is difficult to monitor the amount of Welsh medium education delivered.

This confusion and complexity is reflected in this description, found in an official Estyn (HMI) report on a school in Cardiff: "*Ysgol Gyfun Gymraeg Glantaf*, Cardiff [Glantaf Welsh-medium comprehensive school], is a designated bilingual comprehensive school" (Estyn 2005: 6). The school is thus termed both 'Welsh-medium' and 'bilingual', highlighting the lack of clarity in typology.

The need for research

Although Welsh-medium and bilingual education has flourished in Wales for over 60 years, no comprehensive data or evidence exists regarding the use of different language allocation strategies currently situated in Welsh classrooms. Considering that nearly seventy years have passed since the opening of Ysgol Gymraeg Aberystwyth in 1939 and that little research has been carried out into the actual use of Welsh and English in classrooms by teachers and pupils in teaching and learning, it is timely that the ESRC Centre for Research on Bilingualism in Theory and Practice was established at Bangor University in January 2007.This is the first research centre in the United Kingdom to focus specifically on bilingualism (www.bilingualism.bangor.ac.uk).

Whilst the work of the Centre draws on several disciplines in order to conduct research into the field of bilingualism, one major bilingual education research project will concentrate specifically on bilingual education in the primary and secondary schools of Wales.

This research project — which will be the first comprehensive survey of its kind on methods of bilingual teaching and learning in Welsh schools — will aim to define and analyse different models of bilingual education in Wales. Its main focus will be on the use of Welsh and English with different groups of pupils in a variety of lessons and subject areas across the primary and secondary curriculum.

The project will be in three stages:

1. Surveying and observation of existing classroom practice leading to an initial typology of classroom language allocation;
2. Consultation with practitioners and advisers so as to define optimally effective language allocation strategies;

3.   Production of training materials for the pre-service and in-service education of teachers, to relay optimally effective language allocation strategies in the classroom.

The first stage of the research is to survey and observe existing practices in the use of two languages in the classroom in a purposive sample of a minimum of nine secondary schools and eighteen feeder primary schools in eight Local Education Authorities across Wales (representative of different geographic and sociolinguistic contexts).

A wide variety of approaches are utilized by teachers across Wales — from perpetual code-switching to a more defined planning of usage. The survey will enable us to construct a typology of language allocation. Therefore, the data collected during this first stage of the research will provide evidence for bilingual methodology approaches that:

–   will be cross disciplinary (across subject areas);
–   will be cross sector (primary/secondary schools);
–   takes into account varying ages, gender, social class and intellectual development;
–   takes into account the location of a child on the second language/first language continuum (immersion and heritage language);
–   is relevant to varying language contexts (e.g. English newcomers to Welsh heartland areas; immersion classes where the majority are from English language backgrounds; classes where there is a mixture of L1 and L2 Welsh-speaking children);
–   is relevant to small schools in rural areas (where there can be a wide age-range within one class) and large schools in urban areas (where there is a more favourable teacher-pupil ratio).

That Welsh-medium and bilingual educational practices vary so much across Wales — dependent on a number of variables — means that no one narrow model can be produced to fit all situations. It would be impossible and impractical to construct one overarching typology to encompass the variety of existing practices. Baker (1993b: 15) has emphasised that "the kaleidoscopic variety of bilingual educational practice in Wales makes the production of a simple typology inherently dangerous … No existing typology of bilingual education in Wales captures the full kaleidoscope of colours that exists". Rather, the research in progress aims at creating an initial typology of language allocation — both on a whole-school level and on a classroom level — across a wide spectrum that is representative of different socio-linguistic contexts. This, in turn, will inform the third stage of the project, which will be the designing of models and training materials for teachers and initial teacher training institutions. With reference to the current training of teachers in Wales, the irony of the situation is that they are generally trained to teach through the medium of Welsh, or through the medium of English; yet, the reality is that in the schools where they work, they will be operating through both languages in the classrooms. This research project aims at producing training materials that match the needs of teaching and learning in a variety of bilingual situations across Wales.

Research into bilingual methodology is welcomed by the teaching profession in Wales. Educationalists and researchers over the last decade have emphasised the importance of carrying out qualitative and ethnographic research into "the complexities on the ground in different school settings, particularly the specific communicative challenges facing teachers and learners in classrooms — challenges that stem from particular ways of organising bilingual provision" (Jones and Martin-Jones 2004: 65).

Research methodology

The methodology utilized within this research into bilingual education in the primary and secondary schools of Wales encompasses a number of research instruments:

- semi-structured interviews with headteachers, language co-ordinators, teachers and pupils in primary and secondary schools focusing on whole-school language use and allocation, language use and allocation within individual subjects in classrooms, assessment, language support for different groups of pupils, home/community links, training;
- whole-school observations focusing on the overall Welsh language ethos/environment of the school and classrooms, Welsh language profile of teachers in the school (including assistants, support staff), Welsh language profile of all other staff in the school (e.g. cooks, cleaners), teacher use of both languages with pupils in non-learning activity (e.g. management, discipline), language of the playground, technological use of languages, the use of Welsh language support services (e.g. peripatetic language teachers), implementation of the *Curriculum Cymreig* in the school;
- non-participant observation in classrooms focusing on the language profile of pupils in the classroom, the language(s) used by the teacher when addressing the whole class/groups/individuals, the languages used by the pupils when talking to the teacher/talking together in small groups/talking individually to each other, language teaching and instruction, Content and Language Integrated Learning (CLIL), reasons why teachers and/or pupils switch languages within lessons; strategies in respect of the use of two languages in the classroom (e.g. attempt to separate languages, translation, scaffolding for non-fluent pupils, translanguaging);
- collection of information and evidence on schools, e.g. Estyn (HMI) inspection reports, examination results, school prospectuses (see 'Additional Evidence' later);
- case studies of particular classrooms;
- focus groups/conferences/consultations.

The style of research is to collect the widest possible qualitative and quantitative evidence to elucidate processes and products, with sufficient cross-checking (triangulation) of evidence to ensure security and validity in findings.

Emerging pedagogy

With reference to the aforementioned strategies in respect of the use of two languages in the classroom, it has become evident from the first year of classroom observations that one emerging pedagogy that is increasingly used in developing both Welsh and English language competence of pupils, and which also results in effective content learning, is *translanguaging* (a Welsh term coined by Cen Williams as *trawsieithu*). Baker (2000: 104–105) defines this term as "the hearing or reading of a lesson, a passage in a book or a section of work in one language and the development of the work (i.e. by discussion, writing a passage, completing a work sheet, conducting an experiment) in the other language." Thus 'translanguaging' is more specific than the umbrella term 'concurrent use of two languages'. Baker also points to potential advantages of translanguaging. It may promote a deeper and fuller understanding of the subject matter. In a monolingual context it is possible for students to answer questions or write an essay without fully understanding the subject. Whole sentences and paragraphs can be copied or adapted from a textbook without really understanding them. In a bilingual situation this is less easy. To read and discuss a topic in one language, and then to write about it in another, means that the subject matter has to be properly 'digested' and reconstructed. Translanguaging may help students develop skills in the weaker language. Baker (2003) emphasises that translanguaging is not about code-switching or translating. Rather it is a skill for any actively-bilingual individual and is a natural way of simultaneously developing and reinforcing the two languages, while at the same time consolidating and extending the individual's understanding of the subject area.

During this study (to date) two models of translanguaging are emerging: one that is teacher-controlled (which can be classified as *purposive, constructed, and planned activity* by the teacher) and one that is pupil-controlled/pupil-chosen (which can be classified as *serendipitous, unconstructed, and unplanned activity* by the teacher). In both models, the pupils must have developed both languages sufficiently for curriculum content learning to take place. In one example of the latter, two 15 year old pupils interviewed during a secondary school GCSE science lesson on 'The Human Genome Project' observed that they deliberately chose to translanguage from English to Welsh *'so as to avoid copying the original material from the internet word-for-word in order to fully understand the information conveyed in the English text'*.

Additional evidence

In addition to the evidence gathered by means of the research instruments listed above, use will be made of secondary evidence that will provide further information about the linguistic background of the school and its pupils. This evidence encompasses Estyn (HMI) reports, the school's language policy document, the school's curriculum policy document, and the school's timetable and language allocation across the curriculum.

One example of such evidence — that justifies the research in progress — is mentio-end in a recent Estyn (2008: 22) report on Welsh-medium and bilingual provision for 14–19 learners. After stating that in general there is considerable variation in the quality of bilingual teaching, in those cases where bilingual teaching is not effective, planning and classroom organisation is often not flexible enough to cater for the needs of both Welsh-medium and English-medium learners.

To conclude: The challenges for Welsh-medium and bilingual education

That Welsh-medium and bilingual education in Wales is increasing in its popularity in non-Welsh-speaking areas means that the intake into the sector is becoming much more diverse in nature with more pupils from a wider range of socio-economic, linguistic, and cultural backgrounds than in the past (Estyn 2006: 46). This diverse pupil population — with divergent levels of proficiency in Welsh — poses a challenge to the bilingual provision and its organisation across Wales. Hickey (2001: 469–70) found a similar situation facing the bilingual education system in Ireland. She points to factors which will also characterise Welsh-medium education in the years to come. A balance must be achieved between addressing the language needs of L2 learners and the equally urgent needs of L1 minority language children for active language support and enrichment. The future of minority languages such as Welsh depends on not only raising competence in the language among second language learners, but also on maintaining and promoting its use by Welsh home language speakers and between first and second language children. An added challenge that is becoming more evident recently is the increase in the number of pupils from non-English backgrounds — from a range of ethnicities other than Welsh/White British — into schools in Wales (Welsh Assembly Government 2007b). Not only do these pupils contribute to the diverse social, cultural, and religious aspects of schooling, but careful consideration must also be given to their additional language support needs in both Welsh and English (Brentnall, 2009). With such a diverse linguistic population within Welsh-medium and bilingual schools in Wales, the need for carefully planned Content and Language Integrated Learning (CLIL) is becoming increasingly important in immersion settings (Fortune, Tedick and Walker 2008: 71–96) and can be seen as one of the major challenges for the future training of teachers — both within initial teacher training courses and within in-service training provision.

To summarise, as Welsh-medium and bilingual education continues to become increasingly more diverse and 'kaleidoscopic', the main issues that need to be considered in the strategic planning of the provision to meet the challenges of the twenty first century include the following:

– how to organise Welsh-medium/bilingual provision for pupils with a range of different levels of proficiency in Welsh and English in the same classrooms;

- how to support and develop the Welsh and English of pupils from Welsh-speaking homes;
- how to develop the Welsh and English of pupils from non-Welsh (and non-English) speaking homes;
- how to promote effective interaction between L1 pupils (from Welsh-speaking homes) and L2 pupils (from non-Welsh-speaking homes);
- how to develop teaching strategies that develop and take advantage of pupils' bilingualism;
- how to ensure linguistic continuity and progression from the primary sector to the secondary sector so as to minimise the language loss that occurs as pupils choose not to continue with their education through the medium of Welsh and, in particular, those pupils who followed Welsh as a first language in primary school becoming 'Welsh second language' learners in secondary school (Redknap 2006: 12–14; Baker and Jones 2000; Welsh Language Board 1999, 2000);
- how to promote and foster language transmission that has commenced with language reproduction in the family and/or nursery school (Baker and Jones 1999; Welsh Language Board 2000);
- how to promote the use of Welsh outside the school as "there is also the current danger of Welsh becoming the language of the school, and English the language of the street, screen and shop. Rather than Welsh being a school-only phenomenon, it needs to penetrate an individual's whole way of life, and can be present in everyday active, participatory culture" (Baker 1993b: 28).

If Welsh-medium and bilingual education is to continue to develop and flourish in the twenty first century, it must do so in accordance with the needs and aspirations of those children and parents who choose such an education. As the Chief Executive of Gwynedd County Council expressed, when Gwynedd Local Education Authority's pioneering bilingual education policy was established in 1974: "We bring up children to be bilinguals, not for the sake of language, but for the sake of children" (Baker and Jones 1999:1).

References

Baker, C. 1993a. *Foundations of Bilingual Education and Bilingualism.* Clevedon: Multilingual Matters.

Baker, C. 1993b. Bilingual education in Wales. In *European Models of Bilingual Education,* H. Baetens Beardsmore (ed.), 7–29. Clevedon: Multilingual Matters.

Baker, C. 2000. *The Care and Education of Young Bilinguals: An Introduction for Professionals.* Clevedon: Multilingual Matters.

Baker, C. 2003. Biliteracy and transliteracy in Wales: Language planning and the Welsh National Curriculum. In *Continua of Biliteracy,* N. Hornberger (ed.), 71–90. Clevedon: Multilingual Matters.

Baker, C. 2004. Editorial. *The Welsh Journal of Education*. 13(1): 1–7.

Baker, C. & Jones, S. 1998. *Encyclopedia of Bilingualism and Bilingual Education*. Clevedon: Multilingual Matters.

Baker, C. & Jones, M.P. 1999. *Continuity in Welsh Language Education*. Cardiff: Welsh Language Board

Baker, C. & Jones, M.P. 2000. Welsh language education: A strategy for revitalization. In *Language Revitalization: Policy and Planning in Wales*, C.H. Williams (ed.), 116–137. Cardiff: University of Wales Press.

Brentnall, J. 2009. Minority ethnic additional language learners in Wales. Special issue of *Education Transactions*. Bangor: College of Education and Lifelong Learning.

Davies, J. 1993. *The Welsh Language*. Cardiff: University of Wales Press.

Estyn. 2005. Estyn Report on Ysgol Gyfun Gymraeg Glantaf, Cardiff. (http://www.estyn.gov.uk/inspection_reports/Glantaf_Sec_05.pdf)

Estyn. 2006. *The Annual Report of Her Majesty's Inspector of Education and Training in Wales 2004–2005*. Cardiff: Estyn.

Estyn. 2008. *Welsh-medium and Bilingual Provision for 14–19 Learners*. Cardiff: Estyn.

Fortune, T.W., Tedick. D.J. & Walker, C.L. 2008. Integrated language and content teaching: Insights from the immersion classroom. In *Pathways to Multilingualism: Evolving Perspectives on Immersion Education*, T.W. Fortune & D.J. Tedick (eds.), 71–96. Clevedon: Multilingual Matters.

Gathercole, V.C. & Thomas, E.M. 2005. Minority language survival: Input factors influencing the acquisition of Welsh. In *Proceedings of the 4th International Symposium on Bilingualism*, J. Cohen, K.T. McAlister, K. Rolstad & J. MacSwan (eds.), 852–874. Cascadilla Press.

Gibbons, P. 2002. *Scaffolding Language, Scaffolding Learning: Teaching Second Language Learners in the Mainstream Classroom*. Portsmouth NH: Heinemann.

Hickey, T. 2001. Mixing beginners and native speakers in minority language immersion: Who is immersing whom? In *The Canadian Modern Language Review* 57(3): 443–474.

Johnstone, R. 2002. *Immersion in a Second or Additional Language at School: A Review of the International Research*. Stirling: Scottish CiLT.

Jones, D.V. & Martin-Jones, M. 2004. Bilingual education and language revitalization in Wales: Past achievements and current issues. In *Medium of Instruction Policies: Which Agenda? Whose Agenda?*, W. Tollefson & A. Tsui (eds.), 43–70. Mahwah NJ: Lawrence Erlbaum Associates.

Lewis, W.G. 2006. Welsh-medium primary education: The challenges and opportunities of the twenty-first century. In *Welsh-Medium and Bilingual Education*, Welsh Language Board, 21–35. Bangor: Education Transactions.

Lewis, W.G. 2007. Teaching and learning in bilingual situations in Wales today: An overview of the main issues and consideration". *Mauritius Institute of Education: Journal of Education* 5(1): 21–35.

May, S. 2000. Accommodating and resisting minority language policy: The case of Wales. *International Journal of Bilingual Education and Bilingualism* 3(2): 101–128.

National Assembly for Wales. 2003. *2001 Census of Population: First Results on the Welsh Language*. Statistical Bulletin 22/2003. Cardiff: National Assembly for Wales.

Redknap, C. 2006. Welsh-medium and bilingual education and training: Steps towards a holistic strategy. In *Welsh-Medium and Bilingual Education*, Welsh Language Board, 1–19. Bangor: Education Transactions.

Roberts, D.T. 1998. *The Language of the Blue Books*. Cardiff: University of Wales Press.

Welsh Assembly Government. 2003. *Iaith Pawb: A National Action Plan for a Bilingual Wales*. Cardiff: Welsh Assembly Government.

Welsh Assembly Government. 2007a. *Welsh in Schools 2007*. Statistical Bulletin 63/2007. Cardiff: Welsh Assembly Government.

Welsh Assembly Government. 2007b. *SDR 118–2007 — Schools Census 2007: Provisional Results*. Statistical Directorate. Cardiff: Welsh Assembly Government.

Welsh Language Board. 1999. *Welsh Medium and Bilingual Education in Wales: In Perspective*. Cardiff: Welsh Language Board.

Welsh Language Board. 2000. Language revitalization. The role of the Welsh Language Board. In *Language Revitalization: The Role of the Welsh Language Board in Wales,* C.H. Williams (ed.), 83–115. Cardiff: University of Wales Press.

Welsh Language Board. 2002. *The Welsh Language: A Vision and Mission for 2000–2005*. http://www.byig-wlb.org.uk/english/publications/publications/74.pdf

Williams, I.W. (ed.). 2002. *Gorau Arf: Hanes Sefydlu Ysgolion Cymraeg 1939–2000*. Talybont: Y Lolfa.

Williams, I. W. (ed.). 2003. *Our Children's Language: The Welsh-medium Schools of Wales 1939–2000*. Talybont: Y Lolfa.

Author's address

W. Gwyn Lewis
Coleg Addysg a Dysgu Gydol Oes | College of Education & Lifelong Learning
Prifysgol Bangor University
Safle'r Normal Site
BANGOR
Gwynedd
LL57 2PZ

eds094@bangor.ac.uk

Developments in bilingual Frisian-Dutch education in Friesland

Durk Gorter and Cor van der Meer
University of the Basque Country / Ikerbasque / Fryske Akademy,
Ljouwert/Leeuwarden

This paper focuses on the position and development of the Frisian language in the educational system in Friesland. It discusses the achievements and the research results of special projects in bilingual and trilingual schools. It gives an overview of the language proficiency, attitudes and the new challenges of the education system.

The Frisian language has obtained a presence on all levels of education, although marginal in most cases. Language policy by the government has emphasised the teaching of Frisian in primary schools. The developments over the last decades have not been as remarkable as in other regions. The overall attitudes seem moderately positive, more among the public at large and parents than among teachers and school directors. Research has shown repeatedly that school achievement in Dutch is not affected by bilingual programs and the outcomes for Frisian are more positive. The experiment with trilingual education was received positively, although the outcomes for Frisian and English were not as persuasive as expected.

It is concluded that the position of Frisian is rather weak compared to the other cases in this volume, although the point of departure is relatively favourable in terms of the proportion of speakers in society.

Introduction

Frisian, Dutch and English are the three main languages of the education system in Friesland ('Fryslân'). The province of Friesland is located in the north of the Netherlands. It has almost 650,000 inhabitants and a surface of 3,350 km². The land is typically flat and about half the surface is below sea-level, protected by a huge dike from the North Sea. The administrative territory of the province of Friesland coincides reasonably well with the geographic area where the Frisian language is spoken today. The Frisians were one of the Germanic tribes in contact with the Roman Empire as attested

AILA Review 21 (2008), 87–103. DOI 10.1075/aila.21.07gor
ISSN 1461–0213 / E-ISSN 1570–5595 © John Benjamins Publishing Company

by the historians Pliny and Tacitus. The continuity of the people and their language is contested because of extensive flooding of the area in post-Roman times. Frisian is an Indo-European language that can be dated back to the early Middle-ages when older forms of Frisian, English, Dutch, German and other closely related varieties branched into different West-Germanic languages. These common origins are the reason why Frisian is sometimes referred to as the closest relative of English. Modern Frisian however is much closer to Dutch. The linguistic distance between Frisian and Dutch is small. Although both languages are not mutually comprehensible, it is relatively easy to learn to understand Frisian for a Dutch speaker. The earliest texts of Old Frisian are from the 13th century although the names of several persons and places can be dated back many centuries earlier. Roughly between 1300 and 1500 Old Frisian was the most common language of administration, but other languages were also in use. The scribes, for instance, were multilingual in Frisian, Dutch and Latin (Bremmer 2004). Since the beginning of the 16th century Frisian has had close contact with Dutch after the gradual incorporation of the province into the Republic of the Low Countries and later the Kingdom of the Netherlands. From the beginning of the 16th century new incoming civil servants and traders brought new languages with them, in particular forms of early Dutch. A mixed language variety arose in the seven major towns of Friesland due to intensive language contact (Vries 1997). This so-called 'town Frisian' is still spoken to some extent. In recent years its use has gone down rapidly because it is no longer transmitted between generations and its social prestige has lowered.

At the beginning of the 19th century, Frisian disappeared completely from the schools because the inspectors instructed primary school teachers not to tolerate the 'farmers' Frisian'. As a consequence the schools became completely associated with Dutch (Van der Bij and Valk 2005). During the Romantic period in the 19th century, an organized movement to promote the Frisian language was established. At first the movement was reluctant to introduce Frisian in education. However, in 1907 the provincial authorities created a small provision to teach Frisian outside of school hours. Since then attempts have been made to increase the number of lessons of Frisian and later to introduce bilingual education or to put Frisian in the curriculum as an obligatory subject. These efforts continue until today and have met with moderate success.

The position of Frisian as a spoken language in society has become less strong during the second half of the 20th century. The most important factors that contributed to this development are the general increase in the level of education, and the spread of modern means of telecommunication and transportation. The immigration of Dutch speakers to the province can be added as another factor. Frisian has not been able to obtain a substantial part of the central functions in modern society, a fate it shares with many other minority languages (Extra and Gorter 2008: 24–32). Dutch is the dominant language in society and in education as well. It is taken for granted as the language of communication in all formal domains. However, Frisian is spoken by over half of the population as their first language (approximately 320.000 persons). It is spoken mainly in situations of informal communication in the family, the community and the lower work sphere. Intergenerational transmission of the language is at risk among younger parents (Foekema 2004). The results from language surveys over the past 40 years have shown a remarkable stability for the receptive skills of understanding and reading. The ability to speak Frisian is gradually decreasing, whereas the self-reported skills in writing have increased (Province Fryslân 2007).

Table 1. Percentage of the population competent in Frisian

Skill/year	1967	1980	1994	2007
Understand	97	94	94	94
Read	69	65	64	75
Speak	85	73	74	74
Write	11	10	17	26

(Source: Province Fryslân 2007: 5)

Dutch is known by the whole population of Friesland. All speakers of Frisian are bilingual and many mother tongue speakers are literate in Dutch but cannot write their own language. Dutch is the official state language of the Netherlands and one of the three official languages of Belgium. In both countries together there are almost 20 million speakers. In the Netherlands, newspapers, magazines, books, official publications and documents, or any other written communication, are through the medium of Dutch. In Friesland, there is a modest stream of literary publications in Frisian and a few announcements by the provincial government and some municipalities are in Frisian. The regional newspapers include some items in Frisian, but it amounts to less than 3% of the editorial texts. There is also a modest provision of Frisian radio and television. At the same time the English language obtains an increasingly important position on Dutch television, in advertising and in the linguistic landscape of public space (Cenoz and Gorter 2006). English can no longer be considered to be a foreign language but a second or third language that people are confronted with and get input from every day. Almost all inhabitants of the Netherlands say they can hold a conversation in English and according to the Eurobarometer survey (2005) 87 percent claim to have those skills. This percentage is similar to Sweden and Denmark, and more than double the average of the European Union.

Historically a number of regional variants that are not part of the Frisian language in itself have also been spoken in the territory of the province of Friesland. On the one hand, varieties that have come into being in the 16th century due to the intensified contact between earlier forms of Dutch and Frisian in the more important towns and some of the islands. On the other hand, we find a Low-Saxon dialect in the southeast where the language border does not completely coincide with the administrative border. Those varieties have no written tradition of any importance and they are only exceptionally taught in primary schools. Most of them seem to be declining rapidly, notwithstanding some local cultural interest and a minor degree of lip-service recognition by the local and state authorities in recent years. At the same time the number of foreign languages has increased due to an influx of migrants, refugees and asylum seekers. One study among primary school children in the capital of Leeuwarden found that around 50 different mother tongues were spoken at home (Van der Avoird et al. 2000). The five most common foreign mother tongues were English, Arabic, Kurdish, Hindi and Berber, which together accounted for 50% of all speakers of foreign home languages. These languages, except for English, play a minor role in public life. In general, multilingualism has been on the rise in the province of Friesland in recent years (Gorter, Van der Meer, Riemersma 2008: 192), but the recent change in Dutch educational policy has removed all facilities for teaching migrant languages inside the school system.

The Frisian educational system

The schools in Friesland are completely incorporated into the educational system of the Netherlands. The structural characteristics of the educational system in Friesland are the same. The Dutch system consists of a centralized education policy by the Ministry of Education with the administration and management of schools at the local level. The central state has the power to determine educational arrangements by law for both public and private schools. All schools are governed by a competent authority at the local level. There is a division between public schools (managed by the local government) and private schools (managed by private foundations with a religious base). The state inspectorate has to monitor the practice of education. In the Netherlands the provinces are an intermediate layer of government with no role in educational matters. The province of Friesland is an exception because it has an advisory role concerning the Frisian language in education. This role includes the ruling on exemptions from the obligation to teach Frisian in primary schools. The provincial government has developed a general policy to promote and protect the Frisian language. Education is one of the spearheads of the language policy and thus the provincial government encourages the teaching of Frisian at all levels of education (Plan fan oanpak 2006).

In the Netherlands Dutch is taken for granted as the language of instruction. For the Frisian language a few exceptions have been made in the educational laws. In the province of Friesland the Frisian language has to be a subject in all primary schools, the language also has to be taught in basic education in secondary schools and Frisian has to be offered by the teacher training colleges. At all levels of education the law allows Frisian to be used as a medium of instruction.

Students come from the province of Friesland itself, except for the three institutes for higher tertiary education, which attract a large number of their students from the rest of the Netherlands and from abroad. As there is no university in Friesland, students have to go to a different province to obtain university training.

A brief sketch of the teaching and the use of Frisian, Dutch and other languages for each level of education is given in the rest of this section. By way of introduction summary statistics on the number of pupils involved in the school system in the province of Friesland are presented in Table 2.

Table 2. Summary statistics for education in Friesland

Type of education	Number of students
preschool, incl. day-care	7,500
Primary, incl. special	64,000
Secondary, incl. special	63,000
Higher	17,000
Total	151,500

Data for the school year 2005–2006. Source: adapted from Riemersma and De Jong (2007: 39).

Playgroups and day-care centers (for children of 2–4 years) are mostly privately initiated; they are supervised and partly financed by the local governments. None of the 31 municipalities has developed an explicit language policy for pre-school activities, not even if they have a language policy for other domains. The pre-school organizations are left free in their choice of language. In most centers if children speak Frisian, in principle, they will be responded to in Frisian (except when the teacher cannot speak Frisian). A survey showed that most rural playgroups can be regarded as bilingual, while in most urban playgroups Frisian is only used occasionally (Boneschansker and Le Rütte 2000). Between 2003 and 2007 the number of playgroups and centers for day-care that offer a wholly Frisian or a bilingual play environment for the young child increased from 11 to 55 (Boneschansker 2006: 10). In general, in bilingual centers one of the teachers consistently uses Frisian and another Dutch. The 55 centers cater for approximately 1,275 children, or around 17 percent of the age group.

Primary schools are attended by children of 4–12 years (grades 1–8). All primary schools in Friesland have the obligation to teach Dutch, Frisian and English, the latter in the two highest grades. As far as the teaching of Frisian is concerned there are no differences between public and private schools. The main difference is between the schools in the towns and in the villages. The number of schools that have a school population with a predominantly Frisian language background (over 75%) has decreased substantially over the last 25 years — from 51% in 1981 to 31% in 2005 (Inspectie 2006: 21). About three-quarters of all teachers themselves have a Frisian or a bilingual language background. Of all teachers 94% can speak the language, but only 69% can write Frisian (both percentages are of course higher than the average for the population at large, compare Table 1).

The most common pattern is to teach Frisian for half an hour per week in the lowest grades 1 and 2 and one lesson (30–45 minutes) in grades 3 to 8. The total number of Frisian lessons is approximately 200 hours over a period of 8 years. Compared to the lessons in the Dutch language (usually 5 hours per week) it is very low (Inspectie 2006: 31). The variation in time investment between schools is substantial. Over 40% of schools do not offer Frisian in the first two years. There are also schools that have

2 hours on the curriculum for Frisian as a subject. The number of hours devoted to Frisian seems to depend to a large extent on the decisions of the individual teacher and on his or her language proficiency in Frisian. The overall situation for the teaching of Frisian as a subject has hardly changed since 1980 when Frisian was introduced as a compulsory subject. It seems that schools were not encouraged over the past years to increase the number of hours of Frisian. The position of Frisian is also modest as a medium of instruction for other subjects. In the lowest grades 34% of the schools use some Frisian for creative subjects and physical instruction. In the higher grades the percentage for Frisian as medium of instruction decreases substantially to only 11% in grades 5 to 8 (Inspectie 2006: 32). Overall, about half of all primary schools offer Frisian as a medium of instruction at some stage.

English is taught as a subject for one hour a week in the two highest grades, when the children are 11 and 12 years old. This is a general obligation in the Netherlands. There is no early introduction of English in Friesland so far. At primary level it is exceptional for children to go abroad or to be taught any extra-curricular English classes.

In an effort to stimulate the teaching of Frisian, not English, an experiment with trilingual education was set up in 1997. The educational advisory center (*GCO-Fryslân*, today *CEDIN*), in cooperation with the *Fryske Akademy,* developed a model which is basically bilingual (Ytsma 2000). The main task of the educational advisory center was the development of new learning material for using Frisian as a medium of instruction. Its advisors also organized special training days for teachers of the trilingual schools. The *Fryske Akademy* carried out a longitudinal study. Every year the children were tested on their language abilities and attitudes in Dutch, Frisian and later, English. Seven primary schools located in small villages with a total of approximately 400 pupils participated in the so-called Trilingual Schools Project (Ytsma 2002). In the model 50% of the teaching time is systematically given to Frisian and the other 50% to Dutch. English is introduced as a subject in the 6th grade (one year earlier than in other schools) and in the last two grades, English is used for 20% of the time. In practice pupils have English as medium of instruction during two afternoons per week. The goal is to meet the attainment targets for both Frisian and Dutch to the full extent (which is far from the case in most other schools). Moreover, the pupils have to reach a basic communicative ability in English. The main difference to other schools that use Frisian as medium of instruction is the systematic and equal division of both languages over the teaching time. It is known that other bilingual schools use both languages less systematically. The position of English is distinctive for the experiment (Van Ruijven and Ytsma 2008). The outcomes of the experiment in terms of language proficiency will be discussed below.

After the experiment came to an end in 2006, a network of trilingual schools was established in which two years later 20 schools are participating. The trilingual schools are one of the focal points of provincial language policy for education.

Secondary education has a complex structure in the Netherlands because of the different levels and school types. They are stratified according to three levels of increasing intellectual challenge for the students. All secondary schools have in common a period of 2 to 4 years of basic education (*"basisvorming"*). Its length varies and depends on the school level and the curriculum of each school. The core curriculum contains 15 subjects, but schools are free to decide how much time they want to devote to each subject. The Dutch and English languages are taught as subjects in all schools. In some schools German and French can be chosen as foreign languages. In the '*gymnasium*' Greek and Latin are taught as well. Thus a number of children in a gymnasium in Friesland may be taught no less than seven different languages as a subject.

Frisian is also an obligatory subject in secondary education. However, hardly any attention is paid to continuity between teaching Frisian at primary and at secondary school. Only 62 percent of all the different schools do indeed offer Frisian, some have obtained an exemption and others just do not teach any Frisian (Inspectie 2006: 45). Most schools have limited Frisian to the first two years, for one hour a week which implies those students will receive around 80 hours of instruction in Frisian. For almost all students it will stop there because Frisian is only an optional subject in the higher grades. In the whole province around 70 students take Frisian as a subject for their final exams, which is less than 1%.

Even though there are no legal obstacles to teach through the medium of Frisian it is seldom done. A remarkable outcome of the study of the inspectorate is that 62 percent of the teachers reports to use Frisian in informal contacts with students (Inspectie 2006: 48). In written communications Frisian plays no role.

Mergers in *secondary vocational education* led to the establishment of three large Regional Training Centers, which offer a wide range of courses. Although there is no legal requirement for any subject to be taught, it is rather exceptional when Frisian is taught. There are a few possibilities for taking a subject related to Frisian. For instance, the health sector includes a training course for nurses where Frisian can be chosen as part of the course.

The Regional Training Centers also provide *adult education courses*. Frisian can be used as an element of a literacy course. But most courses make little use of Frisian in their programs. Outside these large centers there is the *Afûk*, an independent educational institute that specializes in Frisian classes for adults. The courses vary from basic courses for learning to understand and read Frisian to more advanced courses in writing and literature. The *Afûk* also has a task in the production and publication of Frisian learning materials and children's books. Each year around 1,000 students attend a Frisian language class. Recently the *Afûk* has started the provision *Edufrysk*, an on-line language course.

At *tertiary level* there are three institutes of professional training in Ljouwert. They offer a wide range of courses. As a rule Dutch is the language of instruction in tertiary education in the Netherlands. All three institutes have a so-called 'language statute' in which the exceptions (e.g. using English or Frisian) are specified. There is a trend to provide more and more courses through the medium of English in order to attract students from abroad. Strictly speaking Frisian is almost always allowed in oral exams or in writing a thesis, but in practice the use of Frisian is exceptional.

Teacher training for primary education is provided by two of the three institutes and teacher training for secondary is provided only by one. Students must follow a Frisian language course during the first two years of their training. Frisian is optional in the third year. Frisian and non-Frisian speaking students are separated in different streams. Even with the limited number of modules most students obtain a certificate which allows them to teach Frisian in primary or secondary school.

Language policy in education

In 2008 for the third time in a row the Dutch government has been severely criticized by the Committee of Experts on the Charter of Regional or Minority Languages (1998) of the Council of Europe. The Charter is part of the legal framework to promote and protect the cultural heritage of languages in Europe (De Bot and Gorter 2005: 613). The main task of the Committee of Experts is to examine the real situation of a minority language and to evaluate if the state is acting according to accepted standards (Committee of Experts 2008: 2). The Committee of Experts points again to the lack of implementation of a consistent policy for the Frisian language, in particular in education. The Committee comes to this conclusion after the evaluation of the third triennial state report of the Netherlands. That periodic report was produced as part of the monitoring process of the European Charter (Ministry of the Interior 2007). The report provides a detailed description of the measures taken to promote and protect the Frisian language and culture in the years 2002 through 2007. On the basis of its findings the Committee of Experts reports to the Committee of Ministers, the highest body of the Council of Europe. The ministers have adopted a number of recommendations for the authorities in The Netherlands. The most important recommendation is to "strengthen the teaching of and in Frisian at all levels of education" (Committee of Ministers 2008). This formulation is a diplomatic way of stating that hardly anything has changed since its last recommendation (Committee of Ministers 2004) or even since its first judgment (Committee of Ministers 2001). The Dutch government has thus been repeatedly criticized for its lack of support for the Frisian language in education. The latest report leads to questions being asked in the Dutch parliament on how the government intends to handle the recommendations (Tweede Kamer 2008). The answers by the minister of the interior point to the possibility of the devolvement of powers in the field of language policy and for Frisian in education, although this proposal and its details first have to be studied by a state commission.

It can be assumed that the Dutch state government did not appreciate the feedback of the Council of Europe; probably it was not seen as an important political problem either. The Frisian language is not high on the agenda of the policy makers in The Hague. According to the study by Hemminga (2000), the ministry of education has held a consistent negative or at most indifferent view towards the Frisian language in education over a period of 70 years. Frisian was introduced in education about 100 years ago when the provincial authorities gave a small grant for the teaching of Frisian outside the curriculum. In the 1920s and 1930s a lobby from Friesland succeeded after many years of pressure to have the general educational law changed in 1937. The word 'Frisian' was avoided on purpose in the text of the law, but it became possible to include a few hours of 'living dialect' in the teaching of the national standard language Dutch. New initiatives for the support of the Frisian language resulted after World War II in an experiment with a small number of bilingual Frisian-Dutch schools. At first those were not legal but only tolerated. After a new change of the law in 1955, it became possible to teach Frisian as a subject in all grades and to use Frisian as a medium of instruction in the three lowest grades. About 20% of all primary schools became bilingual in the 1950s and 1960s. In later years the number declined because the élan and excitement of the post-war years had gradually disappeared. The Frisian movement, supported by all political parties, began to advocate the obligation to teach Frisian as a subject to all primary school children. The state government was reluctant, but in the end consented. Thus, in 1980 Frisian obtained the status of obligatory subject on the curriculum, similar to Dutch, mathematics and other subjects. What seemed like a major triumph for the promotion of Frisian at the time has turned out to be a Pyrrhus victory. The position of Frisian in primary education has remained marginal. By far most schools only teach Frisian for one school-hour a week and not even in all eight grades. Repeated studies by the Inspectorate between 1989 and 2005 show hardly any or no progress, neither in the quantity nor in the quality of teaching Frisian (Inspectie 2006). The designated bilingual schools from the 1950s and 1960s have gradually disappeared in the 1980s. The overall picture that arises from the last inspectorate report shows a great diversity in the ways primary schools pay attention to the Frisian language (Inspectie 2006). A few schools seem to want to avoid Frisian, some use Dutch during the Frisian lessons, others comply only with the minimal legal obligation and put Frisian on the curriculum for one hour a week. Many schools prefer to use the materials provided by the educational advisory service CEDIN and they also like to watch the school television programs. It is a kind of passive and consumerist approach to teaching Frisian. At the other side of the spectrum there is also a number of schools that take Frisian seriously. They have developed a language policy according to which they want to reach the attainment targets for Frisian. In those schools the number of hours on the curriculum is similar to other subjects and the language is used as a medium of instruction as well.

Language attitudes, school achievement and trilingual schools

Over the past fifty years several research projects have investigated the specific language situation in education in Friesland. Almost all studies concern primary education, there are relatively few studies about secondary education or the other levels. The advantages and disadvantages of bilingual education have been investigated most frequently. In a technical sense many Frisian primary schools are bilingual because both the Frisian and Dutch languages are used as a subject and as a medium of instruction, but Dutch clearly prevails. Survey results show that the population at large is positive about Frisian at school, but there is no general support for a bilingual school where Frisian and Dutch are used equally (Gorter and Jonkman 1995). The debate usually circles around the issue of the influence of bilingual education on the acquisition of the standard language. The idea that teaching a minority language impedes the learning of the majority language is widespread. In the 19th century this thought was common. Academic research has challenged this conviction and also refuted the arguments. However, the debate is still relevant in our time (Cummins 2001, Baker 2006, Huss, Camilleri and King 2003).

Attitudes

Several studies have confirmed a strong correlation between a Frisian language background and having a more favorable attitude towards the Frisian language than speakers with a Dutch language background (Pietersen 1967, Gorter et al 1984, Lutje Spelberg and Postma 1995, Ytsma 1995).

The population survey in the mid-nineties showed that 87 percent of Frisian speakers attach a lot of importance to the Frisian language, whereas among Dutch speakers in Friesland this was 34 percent (Gorter and Jonkman 1995: 35). These differences between the language groups do not come as a surprise. There exists little open resistance against Frisian, but there is a lot of implicit degradation of Frisian. Students in teacher training with Frisian as the first language also appreciate bilingualism and trilingualism more than students with Dutch as their first language (Benedictus 2005). Attitudes towards Dutch, Frisian and English among students in the first year of teacher training college were investigated. It was found that unfavorable attitudes towards the three languages are rare, just a few students expressed negative opinions on Frisian and on English, and no students at all held negative opinions towards Dutch (Ytsma 2007: 157). The outcome confirmed that students are more positively predisposed towards their own language. Ytsma (2007: 162) proposed a language awareness program for these prospective teachers to change their attitudes. Ytsma also reported results where language attitudes had indeed changed, but he warned against too much optimism for such change.

De Jager (2004) investigated the language attitudes and reading pleasure of Frisian primary school students. Only 16 percent of the students held a positive attitude towards reading Frisian texts. One quarter of the students indicated to read a Frisian book from time to time.

In a longitudinal study Van der Bij and Valk (2005) looked into the effect of a special project to promote positive attitudes towards Frisian in secondary schools. They measured language attitudes before and after the measures were implemented as part of the project and they also included control schools. Their conclusion is that more students take the exam for Frisian at the project schools, but the intended effect of improvement of the attitudes towards Frisian did not take place. The attitudes of the teachers involved in the project had improved somewhat. According to the researchers the project to promote Frisian took place in the margins of the secondary schools and the involvement of most teachers was minimal. They compare the difficult implementation of Frisian in secondary school with the dancing procession in Echternach: three steps forward and two steps backward.

The surveys carried out by the inspectorate showed that almost all parents have a positive or neutral attitude towards the Frisian language in general. The parents investigated agreed to 70 percent with the fact that schools pay attention to Frisian, and 12 percent wants the school to "do much more about Frisian". The remaining 18 percent do not consider Frisian at school to be important. The directors of schools were asked to estimate the opinions of parents on the same item. The result was that the directors severely underestimated the favorable opinions of the parents towards Frisian (Inspectie 2006).

School achievement in Dutch and Frisian

Already in the 1970s Wijnstra (1976) concluded after an elaborate study on the proficiency in Dutch at the end of primary school that there are no differences between Frisian speaking children in Friesland and Dutch speaking children from another similar province where no minority language is spoken. Although it was not included in the testing, he observed that children in bilingual schools had also learned to read and write in Frisian.

Almost 20 years later De Jong and Riemersma (1994) investigated proficiency in Dutch again. This time they also included elaborate testing for the proficiency in Frisian. Their approach took the formal attainment targets for both languages into consideration, which were identical at the time. The Frisian speaking and the Dutch speaking students reached the same level of Dutch language proficiency as students in other parts of the Netherlands. The level of proficiency in Frisian was below the attainment targets. On the basis of their outcomes the authors propose to introduce a more balanced bilingual model to improve proficiency in Frisian.

In a large scale longitudinal study, Van Ruijven (2003, 2004) investigated educational results of primary and secondary school children in the province of Friesland. She focused on the attainment levels for Dutch language and mathematics compared to the national Dutch average and in particular the provinces of Drenthe and Limburg. She found that at the end of primary school on average students in Friesland lag behind the national averages — a finding that is confirmed by other studies (Van Langen and Hulsen 2001, De Jager, Klunder and Ytsma 2002). One effect of this retardation is that children from Friesland continue in secondary education more on the lower strata (as was mentioned before secondary education is stratified according to three levels) and thus they later also participate less in higher education. Van Ruijven (2004) goes to great lengths to find explanatory variables why pupils fall behind. She starts with a descriptive study of differences between school children in Friesland and in the other two provinces. Thereafter she carries out a multi-level analysis to determine which variables do have a statistically significant contribution. She looks at individual and household characteristics (gender, age, number of siblings, motivation to excel, intelligence, household composition, socio-economic background, etc.) and finds relationships that have been found before for Dutch language scores. She also looks at characteristics of teachers and of schools (years of experience, didactic behavior, time spent on mathematics, size, denomination, etc.) and finds some effects for the scores for mathematics. In the public debate surrounding the "alarming backwardness" in education, some opinion leaders point to the Frisian language as a causal factor. They play on a popular stereotype surrounding minority languages and bilingualism as a source for problems in education. Since this argument keeps coming back in the public discourse, Van Ruijven (2004: 152, 178) deals explicitly with these arguments against the Frisian language. Language background is a non-effect according to her model. The children with Frisian as their mother tongue do not score differently from children with Dutch as mother tongue when tested on Dutch language or on mathematics.

Trilingual education

As we saw, De Jong and Riemersma (1994) concluded from their study that the targets for Frisian were not attained, nor those for English. In the ensuing discussion in the 1990s the recommendation was made to develop a new bilingual model. The outcome was the Trilingual Schools Project, which was developed in such a way that the attainment targets for Dutch, Frisian and English would be reached. In practice it is predominantly a bilingual model where for the first six grades (4–10 year-olds) Dutch and Frisian are taught an equal number of hours as a subject and both are also used for half of the teaching time as medium of instruction. In the final two years of primary school English is added as a third language, both as a subject and as an instruction language, for about 20 per cent of the time. The difference of the trilingual schools to other primary schools in Friesland is in the substantially larger amount of time taught through Frisian, at least compared to the average of all primary schools. Moreover, English is not only a subject as it is in all primary schools, but also for a limited amount of time used as a medium of instruction (Gorter 2005).

The Fryske Akademy carried out a longitudinal research project to investigate the results of the Trilingual Schools Project. Deelstra and Ytsma (2005) compared the language background, language attitudes, vocabulary and reading skills in Frisian and in Dutch of students from the experimental trilingual schools and the control schools. Reading skills, vocabulary and attitudes hardly differed at all, but the students in the experimental schools scored higher on technical reading skills in Frisian. The difference was largest for Dutch speaking children. Van Ruijven and Ytsma (2008) summarize the end results for the eight years of the longitudinal study. Language proficiency for Dutch, Frisian and English has been tested in different ways in the 7 experimental schools as well as in the 10 control schools. The students in groups 7 and 8, at the end of primary school, were assessed for Dutch comprehensive reading, technical reading and spelling. It turned out that the differences between the experimental and the control schools were not statistically significant for any of the three tests of Dutch literacy.

Similar tests were used to assess proficiency in Frisian. Although there are some positive differences in reading comprehension scores for the students of the experimental schools, those are not significant. Statistical significant differences were found for technical reading skills and for the spelling of Frisian. The outcomes demonstrate that the children at the experimental schools score on average higher on Frisian literacy skills. Proficiency in literacy skills for English has been assessed by testing for reading comprehension, listening comprehension and vocabulary. The differences between the schools are very small and are statistically not significant. The aim of the Trilingual schools to obtain better results in English proficiency was not fulfilled.

The oral use of Frisian, Dutch and English was studied in detail by Van der Meij (2008). She investigated two grades in one experimental school of the Trilingual Schools Project. She compared this experimental school to one ordinary bilingual school. Both schools are small and each is located in a small village in the countryside where Frisian is the dominant language of communication. Of all 40 children that participated in the study 28 (70%) had Frisian as their mother tongue, which is about the same as for the population of the local communities where they live (Province Fryslân 2007: 22).

Children were tested on their oral proficiency in each of the three languages separately. They were given the task of telling a short story with three different sets of 6 pictures (see Bos 1997). Each child was first tested in its L1 (Frisian or Dutch), than in its L2 and finally in the L3 (English). The data were transcribed and analyzed for pauses, pause fillers, repetitions, transfer, neologisms, prompts, MLU (Mean Length of Utterance), TTR (Type Token Ratio), and errors. She investigated in particular degree of fluency and vocabulary. Van der Meij (2008: 51–52) could not confirm her hypothesis that children in the experimental school are more proficient in Frisian than the children of the ordinary bilingual school. There were also no differences for the Dutch language, as had been predicted. The results did not indicate that the children in the trilingual school are more proficient in English than the children in the bilingual school. These results are similar to those reported in the investigation of literacy skills by the Fryske Akademy (Van Ruijven and Ytsma 2008).

Conclusions

There are several reasons why the position of Frisian in education is rather weak. First of all Frisian is not perceived as an important condition for socio-economic success. Except for some specific jobs it is not necessary to be literate in Frisian. Another reason is the social position of Frisian in society. Outside and inside the schools the authorities display in their language behavior that Frisian is not important. As a consequence, Frisian lessons are not taken seriously. Frisian is usually not being graded for the report card and when it is, it does not count for much (Van der Bij and Valk 2005).

The point of departure for Frisian as a minority language is favorable in terms of the relative number of speakers and the basic positive attitudes among the population, at least compared to many other minority languages in Europe (Nelde, Strubell and Williams 1996). Frisian may still have the potential of becoming a generally accepted language in the schools side by side with Dutch and partly English. The severe criticism of the Inspectorate (Inspectie 2006) and the Committee of Experts (2008) of the Council of Europe may have some influence to move the position of the state government. The current agreement on the Frisian language between the state and the provincial authorities dates from 2001 and a new formal agreement is due by 2010.

Recently the Dutch state government seems to have changed its position and now it could devolve its powers and financial means concerning Frisian language teaching to the regional and local authorities. It could create the opportunity for the provincial government to seriously strengthen its policy towards support for Frisian in education.

Language policy development is a steady process and implementation of the language plans is even slower. In comparison to several other minority languages in Europe, bilingual Frisian-Dutch education seems attainable. Attitudes of parents are more favorable towards Frisian than the school directors think. To add a good dose of English to the language mix would certainly help, as trilingual education among European minority languages is growing in importance (Cenoz and Gorter 2005: 2–3).

The way Frisian is taught in schools reflects the position which the Frisian language has in society at large. Schools usually play a conservative role and seldom work for the emancipation of a minority language such as Frisian. However, if children are to become fluent in both languages at the end of their schooling period, a substantial change is needed. In Friesland as elsewhere multilingualism in society is increasing. Many children no longer have only Frisian, only Dutch or only a dialect as their home language. Today many children come from mixed-language families. The language background of students becomes more heterogeneous. The school will have to take the diversity into consideration and educational practice becomes more complicated. The challenge will be to incorporate language diversity in an acceptable manner. Comparing Frisian in education to other European minority languages continues to be an interesting topic for studies into multilingual education.

Acknowledgement

This article has been written as part of the contribution to the European 6th Framework network of excellence *Sustainable Development in Diverse World* (sus.div).

References

Baker, C. 2006. *Foundations of Bilingual Education and Bilingualism,* 4th edn. Clevedon: Multilingual Matters.

Benedictus, J. 2005. Over Fries gesproken… Een onderzoek naar taalhouding en drietaligheid bij Pabo-studenten in Fryslân. MA thesis, Rijksuniversiteit Groningen.

Bos, P. 1997. *Development of Bilingualism: A Study of Moroccan Children in the Netherlands.* Tilburg: Tilburg University Press

Boneschansker, E. & Le Rütte, M. 2000. *Pjuttepraat. Friestaligheid in peuterspeelzalen en kinderdagverblijven.* Ljouwert: Economisch Bureau Coulon.

Boneschansker, E. 2006. Evaluaasje Sintrum Frysktalige Berneopfang. Ljouwert: BBO.

Bremmer, R.H. 2004. *Hir is eskriven: Lezen en schrijven in de Friese landen rond 1300.* Hilversum: Verloren.

Cenoz, J. & Gorter, D. 2005. Trilingualism and minority languages in Europe. *International Journal of the Sociology of Language* 171: 1–5.

Cenoz. J. & Gorter, D. 2006. The linguistic landscape and minority languages. *International Journal of Multilingualism* 3(1): 67–80.

Committee of Experts 2008. Report of the Committee of Experts on the Charter: Application of the Charter in the Netherlands. ECRML (2008)8. Strasbourg, 9 July 2008. Council of Europe.

Committee of Ministers 2001. Recommendation of the Committee of Ministers of the Council of Europe on the application of the Charter by the Netherlands. Application of the Charter in the Netherlands. ECRML (2001)1. Strasbourg, 20 September 2001.

Committee of Ministers 2004. Recommendation of the Committee of Ministers of the Council of Europe on the application of the Charter by the Netherlands. Application of the Charter in the Netherlands, 2nd monitoring cycle. ECRML (2004)8. Strasbourg, 16 December 2004.

Committee of Ministers 2008. Recommendation of the Committee of Ministers of the Council of Europe on the application of the Charter by the Netherlands. Application of the Charter in the Netherlands, 3rd monitoring cycle. RecChL (2008)4. Strasbourg, 9 July 2008.

Cummins, J. 2001. Bilingual children's mother tongue: Why is it important for education? Online resource: http://www.iteachilearn.com/cummins/mother.htm, accessed 22 Sept 2008.

De Bot, C. & Gorter, D. 2005. "A European perspective on heritage languages", *Modern Language Journal* 89: 612–616.

De Jager, B., Klunder, M. & Ytsma, J. 2002. *Naar school in Smallingerland. Onderzoek naar schoolprestaties in de gemeente Smallingerland.* Fryske Akademy: Ljouwert.

De Jager, B. 2004. *Leesbegrip, leesplezier en de Friese taalnorm.* Amsterdam: Stichting Lezen.

De Jong, S. & Riemersma, A.M.J. 1994. *Taalpeiling yn Fryslân; Onderzoek naar de beheersing van het Fries en Nederlands aan het einde van de basisschool.* Leeuwarden: Fryske Akademy.

Deelstra, H. & J. Ytsma. 2005. Onderzoeksresultaten groep 3 en 4 project Drietalige Basisschool; onderzoeksresultaten groep 5 en 6 project Drietalige Basissschool. Leeuwarden: Fryske Akademy (internal report).

Eurobarometer 2006. Europeans and their languages, Special Eurobarometer 243 — Wave 64.3 European Commission http://ec.europa.eu/education/languages/pdf/doc631_en.pdf

European Charter for Regional or Minority Languages (1998) *Explanatory Report.* (ETS no. 148) Strasbourg: Council of Europe. http://conventions.coe.int/Treaty/EN/Reports/Html/148. htm, Accessed 22 Sept 2008.

Extra, G. & Gorter, D. 2008. The constellation of languages in Europe: An inclusive approach. In *Multilingual Europe: Facts and Policies*, G. Extra & D. Gorter (eds), 3–60. Berlin: Mouton de Gruyter.

Foekema, H. 2004. Overdracht van de Friese taal. Onderzoek in opdracht van Omrop Fryslân. Amsterdam: TNS/NIPO.

Gorter, D., Jelsma, G.H., van der Plank, P.H. & de Vos, K. 1984. *Taal yn Fryslân — ûndersyk nei taalgedrach en taalhâlding yn Fryslân*, Leeuwarden: Fryske Akademy.

Gorter, D. & Jonkman, R.J.. 1995. *Taal yn Fryslân op 'e nij besjoen.* Leeuwarden: Fryske Akademy.

Gorter, D. 2005. Three languages of instruction in Fryslân. *International Journal of the Sociology of Language* 171: 57–73.

Gorter, D., Van der Meer, C. & Riemersma, A. 2008. Frisian in the Netherlands. In *Multilingual Europe: Facts and Policies,* G. Extra & D. Gorter (eds), 185–206. Berlin: Mouton de Gruyter.

Hemminga, P. 2000. *Het beleid inzake unieke regionale talen.* Leeuwarden: Fryske Akademy.

Inspectie 2001. Het onderwijs Fries in op de basisscholen in Friesland...de stand van zaken. Den Haag: SDU.

Huss, L., Camilleri, A. & King, K. (eds). 2003. *Transcending Monolingualism. Linguistic Revitalisation in Education.* Lisse: Swets and Zeitlinger.

Inspectie 2006. Inspectie van het Onderwijs — De kwaliteit van het vak Fries in het basisonderwijs en het voortgezet onderwijs in de provincie Fryslân. Utrecht: Inspectie van het Onderwijs.

Lutje Spelberg, H.C. & Postma, B. 1995. Taalattitudes in een tweetalige situatie. *It Beaken* 57(1): 30–43.

Ministry of the Interior 2007. The Netherlands: Frisian. European Charter for Regional or Minority Languages 2002–2007. Third State report on the measures taken by the Netherlands with regard to the Frisian language and culture. The Hague: Ministry of the Interior and Kindom Relations.

www.coe.int/t/dg4/education/minlang/Report/PeriodicalReports/NetherlandsPR3_en.pdf [Accessed 22 Sept 2008.]

Nelde, P., Strubell, M. & Williams, G. 1996. *Euromosaic: The Production and Reproduction of the Minority Language Groups in the European Union.* Luxemburg: Office for Official Publications of the European Communities.

Pietersen, L. 1969. *De Friezen en hun taal.* Drachten: Laverman.

Plan fan oanpak 2006. Plan fan oanpak Frysk yn it ûnderwiis. Ljouwert: Provinsje Fryslân.

Province Fryslân 2007. Rapportaazje fluchhifking Fryske taal, Leeuwarden/Ljouwert: Provinsje Fryslân.

Riemersma, A.M.J. & De Jong, S. 2007. *Frisian. The Frisian Language in Education in the Netherlands*, 4th edn. Ljouwert: Mercator Education [Regional Dossiers Series]. On-line at www.mercator-research.eu, accessed 22 Sept 2008.

Tweede Kamer 2008. Vragen gesteld door leden der kamer, met daarop door de regering gegeven antwoorden. Vergaderjaar 2007–2008, nr 3316, 6757–6759. Den Haag.

Van der Avoird, T., Bontje, D., Broeder, P., Extra, G., Muis, R. & Peijs, N. 2000. *Meertaligheid in Leeuwarden. De status van allochtone talen thuis en op school.* Tilburg /Utrecht: Babylon/ Sardes.

Van der Bij, J. & Valk, R.W. 2005. *Fries in het voortgezet onderwijs: een Echternachse processie. Een evaluatieonderzoek naar de effecten van het project Op weg naar 'Fries als examenvak in het voortgezet onderwijs'.* Sneek: Migg.

Van der Meij, M. 2008. Mondelinge taalvaardigheid op de Trijetalige skoalle. MA thesis, Free University Amsterdam.

Van Langen, A. & Hulsen, M. 2001. Prestaties van leerlingen en het gebruik van Fries als voertaal op basisscholen in Fryslân. Nijmegen: ITS.

Van Ruijven, E.C.M. 2003. *Voorsprong of achterstand? Onderzoek naar het onderwijsniveau van de Friese leerlingen in het basisonderwijs en voortgezet onderwijs.* Leeuwarden: Fryske Akademy.

Van Ruijven, E.C.M. 2004. *Onderwijseffectiviteit in Fryslân. Onderzoek naar de omderwijsresultaten van de leerlingen en de kwaliteit van het basisonderwijs en voortgezet onderwijs in Fryslân.* Leeuwarden: Fryske Akademy.

Van Ruijven, E.C.M. & Ytsma, J. 2008. *Trijetalige skoalle yn Fryslân. Onderzoek naar de opbrengsten van het drietalige onderwijsmodel in Fryslân.* Leeuwarden: Fryske Akademy.

Vries, O. 1997. From Old Frisian to Dutch: The elimination of Frisian as a written language in the sixteenth century. In *Language Minorities and Minority Languages*, B. Synak & T. Wicherkiewicz (eds), 239–244. Gdansk: Wydawnictwo Uniwersytetu Gdanskiego.

Wijnstra, J.M. 1976. *Het onderwijs aan van huis uit Friestalige kinderen.* 's Gravenhage: SDU.

Ytsma, J. 1995. *Frisian as First and Second Language.* Leeuwarden: Fryske akademy.

Ytsma, J. 2001. "Towards a typology of trilingual primary education". *International Journal of Bilingual Education and Bilingualism* 4(1): 11–23.

Ytsma, J. 2004. Eén school, drie talen: Drietalig basisonderwijs in Fryslân. In *Jong geleerd is oud gedaan. Talen leren in het basisonderwijs*, R. Aarts, P. Broeder & A. Maljers (eds) 111–119. Den Haag: Europees Platform voor het Nederlandse Onderwijs.

Ytsma, J. 2007. Language use and language attitudes in Friesland. In *Multilingualismin European Bilingual Contexts (Language Use and Attitudes)*, D. Lasagabaster & A.Huguet (eds), 144–163. Clevedon: Multilingual Matters.

Author's address

Durk Gorter, University of the Basque Country/Ikerbasque
Cor van der Meer, Fryske Akademy, Ljouwert/Leeuwarden

Mailing address:
FICE, Un Basque Country
Tolosa Hiribidea 70, 20018 Donostia/San Sebastian
Basque Country, Spain

d.gorter@ikerbasque.org

Postlude

Colin Baker

Introduction

It is salutary to remember that, four or five decades ago, European minority languages were of little interest. Minority languages in Europe have only recently arrived on the academic landscape. Yet, they are now of major interest across a variety of disciplines.

That minority languages in Europe are now a key interest is not due to simple or single effects, reactions, events or leadership. There is a set of complex, interacting and debatable reasons for the growth of international interest in the minority languages of Europe.

For some people, the rise of interest in European minority languages derives from moves away from nation-states and nationalism and is a reaction against the negative attitudes to minority peoples, religions, cultures, ethnicity and languages that scarred Europe before and during the Second World War. For others, the roots lie in the Civil Rights Movement since the 1960s, with its understanding of inequality, racism and human rights that now encompasses language rights for minority groups and individuals. Other academics have accentuated the global ethnic revival (Fishman, 1999). Those in Europe have witnessed the growth of Europeanization with dimensions as broad as politics, business, sport, education, culture, and not least the growing interest in the languages of Europe.

European Language Planning

Whatever is the equation of the rise of interest in European minority languages, part of this growing interest has been the rise of successful language planning in Europe. In the Basque country, Catalonia, Ireland, Wales, Friesland, and many other parts of Europe, there has been the growth of central government, local government and regional language planning aimed at the revitalisation and sometimes salvation or resurrection of minority languages. While many other parts of the world also undertake language planning in a formal or informal manner, it is arguably Europe that has developed, both centrally and regionally, sophisticated but grounded schemes to preserve the minority languages of Europe.

AILA Review 21 (2008), 104–110. DOI 10.1075/aila.21.08bak
ISSN 1461–0213 / E-ISSN 1570–5595 © John Benjamins Publishing Company

In Europe, in a variety of countries, language planning for the revitalisation of minority languages involves a complex equation of:

1. status language planning to embed that language within as many public and private institutions as possible, and to ensure modernity of use e.g. in the mass media;
2. usage or opportunity language planning to facilitate both the integrative use of the language and its attendant culture in areas such as leisure, sport and as many social networks as possible, and also the instrumental use of a language in the economy, for example in the workplace, in employment and education;
3. corpus language planning that attempts to achieve linguistic standardisation through, for example, the use of published dictionaries, and a common language of education at school and in mass media. Such corpus language planning may also attempt to achieve a modern everyday language to ensure continuous evolution and modernisation of the language;
4. acquisition language planning — possibly the essential foundation of all elements of language planning — by encouraging family language reproduction, early childhood use of the minority language in pre-school nurseries, bilingual education from pre-school and for as long as possible, and adult language learning.

Success stories in Celtic countries, Spain, Scandinavia and elsewhere in Europe demonstrate that these four components of language planning are required holistically, interactively and integratively to build a secure future for any minority language (Baker, 2006).

The tide of minority language history in Europe in the last century indicates that there is constant ebb and flow. No minority language is safe. That more status and attention is being given by scholars and researchers to European minority languages does not predicate their use, particularly by younger generations, in homes, in schools, in shops, on the street and on the screen. Against the forces of, for example, industrialisation, urbanisation, ease of transport links, ease of travel, mass media, the decline of rural communities and the growth of virtual communities, the rising status of global languages such as English and Spanish, and many other factors affecting the status of minority languages, the future of European minority languages is neither secure, settled or predictable.

European Minority Language Education

The role of minority language education and bilingual education in the revitalisation of European minority languages cannot be doubted. While a combination of home, community and religion can occasionally be sufficient for language maintenance, in most European language contexts, religion is no longer a major component in language planning or language revival. Bilingual education then becomes an essential but insufficient condition for language revitalisation.

Increasing emphasis has been placed on parents in language revitalisation or maintenance. The inter-generational transmission of minority languages has come to be regarded as an essential foundation in reproducing the language in the new generations. Parents and a local language community, by themselves, may be insufficient, despite high levels of enthusiasm and encouragement, to maintain a minority language across generations. The transmission of the minority language within the family provides a potential. Unless that potential is built on by continued participation in the minority language in later years (e.g. in employment, social networks, mass media), then the building will have no foundation. The potential has to be realized to the extent that the minority language is lived and not just loved, activated in everyday life and not just a passive ideal.

Not only is the family a key and possibly crucial element in language maintenance and revitalisation, but bilingual education takes over the baton from the family by heightening levels of oral and literacy competence in the minority language. Such education has the function of producing more minority language speakers by enabling majority language speakers to become bilingual.

Thus minority language education has an important function both for children from language minority and for those from language majority homes. For the former group, education reinforces early language learning, builds oracy and literacy, enhances curriculum achievement and, where possible, aids employability. For the latter group, bilingual education provides the benefits and advantages of bilingualism: communication, cultural, cognitive, character, curriculum and cash.

There has been a growth of European bilingual education for both minority and majority language children. This sits within a growing consensus of academic and public opinion that recognises the advantages that education in two or more languages bequeaths. We have moved from a parochial fear that bilingual education would result in less achievement to a European belief that education through two or more languages is enhancing and emancipating — an investment for children's futures (Johnstone, 2002). The multilingual capacity of the brain, the benefits to the cognitive system from bilingualism, and the strong evidence that bilingual education is effective, are messages slowly filtering through to politicians and the public alike. Bilingual education in Europe is growing from a small acorn to a sturdy but still young oak tree.

Bilingual education is not just for language revitalisation. It also fits the long tradition in Europe of child-centredness, of emancipating and broadening the lives of children. Being child-centred requires us to establish effective models and practices in bilingual education. We seem to be witnessing a change from effective models to effective practices. We have been through an era when we discussed and researched different models of bilingual education. The future for European bilingual education is perhaps moving away from the simplicity of typologies of bilingual education to engaging with optimal classroom dual language practices that maximise growth and gains for individual children.

A bilingual education typology is a valuable starting point for a specification of key components around which school systems differ, and which locate varying aims, strategies and politics. The current bilingual education literature is replete with models such as Canadian immersion, US Dual Language schools, Heritage Language Education, European Schools, and CLIL. Perhaps it is time to move on. What may better engage policy makers, practitioners, parents and the public is to profile key issues in choices about provision and practice in bilingual education. Some of these will now be briefly outlined as the key decisions in bilingual schools for European minority languages.

1.   **The language profile of children**
A first component around which bilingual schools differ is the type of child attending that school. When a majority language child learns a new language, the home language is unlikely to be replaced by a new school language. In such an additive language context, the child becomes bilingual or multilingual at no expense to their first language. In contrast, minority language children may experience bilingual education that encourages the fruition of their minority language as well as the development of one or more majority languages.

A bilingual school may have a mixture of majority and minority language children, so that the language experience within the school may be different for children of different home backgrounds. In Celtic bilingual schools, one classroom may contain a combination of English first language children and children from homes where Irish, Gaelic, Manx Gaelic or Welsh is the first language. Immersion and heritage language models are combined within one classroom and one school.

2.   **The language balance of children**
This first component leads on to the language balance of the children within a classroom. For example, are all or most of the children from a language majority background? Is there an attempt to achieve a balance between majority and minority language children? Are most or all of the children from language minority homes? Are such children from indigenous, or long-standing or recent immigrant language homes and communities?

This is particularly important, not only in teaching strategies, but also in the status of languages within schools. Researching in Ireland, Hickey (2001) found that, in mixed language classrooms, children from minority language homes tended to switch to English. Such children had less language effect on majority language speakers than English-only speakers had on Irish speakers.

This suggests that the numerical balance of minority language native speakers and learners of a minority language is important, probably being tilted to a predominance of minority language speakers. Classrooms may have a mixture of majority language speakers who are learning through the minority language and native speakers of that minority language. This can mean two different language agendas: minority language speakers acquiring the high-status majority language; majority language speakers acquiring the minority language. The language balance of the classroom is important in achieving such dual aims.

3.   The balance in the use of languages in the classroom

A third component in bilingual education is the balance in the use of two or more languages in the school and classroom. There are a number of sub-components, for example the relative amount of use of two or more languages on walls, in announcements, in non-curriculum activities such as school assemblies, and in the language of the playground, as well as the language of the classroom. In the classroom, what is the balance between the use of two languages?

Typically, in bilingual education, as children move through the grades, less use is made of the minority language and more use is made of the majority language. However, some heritage language schools maintain a strong balance towards the minority language throughout the elementary, even secondary (high school) curriculum. This is to attempt to counter-balance the higher status and use of the majority language outside the school. However, literacy in the majority language is typically regarded as essential.

4.   The allocation of languages in the curriculum

A key and sometimes controversial issue is: what curriculum areas, subjects and topics are taught through the majority and minority language? For example, are mathematics and science only taught through the majority language? What role is given to the minority language in 'modern' pursuits such as computing and in less literacy-based areas (e.g. sports, craft and design technology)? The preference is sometimes to teach mathematics and science in the majority language. This may send signals to the children that the majority language has more functional and prestigious value. The minority language may be perceived to have a restricted usage that connects more with the past than the present, with heritage and history rather than modernity and progression.

5.   The language profile of school personnel

The next component concerns the language profile (and hence role models) of teachers, teacher support staff, administrative staff and Head teachers/Principals. Key issues include: to what extent are such staff bilingual or multilingual? Do such staff use both of their languages and encourage children to do the same? Or does the school hire minority language personnel who use only the majority language in school and thus become 'internal colonisers'?

6.   Teacher Training for a bilingual classroom

Training teachers to work in the bilingual environment, and particularly to use both languages in a well-designed manner in the classroom, is internationally quite rare. For example, training teachers to allocate two or more languages within the same time period (cf Williams' (2000) 'translanguaging' notion of input (e.g. reading) in one language with output (e.g. writing) in a different language) is quite rare in teacher training. Emphasis is often placed on teachers establishing working relationships with minority language homes and communities.

7. The language of curriculum resources

The next component concerns the nature of curriculum resources. Are most curriculum materials experienced by children only in the majority language (e.g. science and mathematics textbooks)? How plentiful, professionally produced, high-quality are the resources produced for minority language content areas? Are the minority language materials mostly home-produced, local and dated? How is the minority language represented when instruction is aided by modern technology, for example use of the World Wide Web and e-learning?

8. Parental Inclusion

Home–school collaboration is typically a major dimension of bilingual school effectiveness. Regular two-way communication can ensure a synthesis and harmonization in bilingual and biliteracy development (e.g. parents helping their child to read and write in both the majority and minority language). Parents can also become partners with the teachers. Parents can be encouraged to bring their 'funds of knowledge' into the classroom, to extend the curriculum (Moll, 1992). For example, parents are repositories of family and community history and heritage, wisdom and cultural understandings, and can share these in the classroom.

Conclusion

While bilingual education may an essential but insufficient component in the revitalization of European minority languages, alongside family language reproduction it is a crucial production line for new speakers of a minority language, a means of developing that language into maturity in young people, and a way of developing enculturation, communication, cognition and employability in that minority language. Bilingual education is thus close to being crucial in language planning.

By itself, it produces a potential, not a finished product. It produces the potential for engagement in a minority language beyond the school: social networks, leisure and employment, for example. That potential may wither on the vine; only years later may it be activated. Alternatively, it may result in aiding language revitalization at a societal level, and enhancement at the individual level. Two languages therefore have double value.

References

Baker, C., 2006. *Foundations of Bilingual Education and Bilingualism,* 4th ed. Clevedon: Multilingual Matters.

Fishman, J. A. (ed.). 1999. *Handbook of Language and Ethnic Identity.* Oxford: OUP.

Hickey, T. 2001. Mixing beginners and native speakers in minority language immersion: Who is immersing whom? *Canadian Modern Language Review* 57(3): 443–474.

Johnstone, R. 2002. *Immersion in a Second or Additional Language at School: A Review of the International Research*. Stirling (Scotland): Scottish Centre for Information on Language Teaching. http://www.scilt.stir.ac.uk/pubs.htm

Moll, L.C. 1992. Bilingual classroom studies and community analysis. *Educational Researcher* 21(2), 20–24.

Williams, C. 2000. Welsh-medium and bilingual teaching in the further education sector. *International Journal of Bilingual Education and Bilingualism* 3(2): 129–148.

Access to online full text

Ingenta *connect*

John Benjamins Publishing Company's journals are available in online full-text format as of the volume published in 2000. Some of our journals have additional (multi-media) information available that is referred to in the articles.

Access to the electronic edition of a volume is included in your subscription. We offer a pay-per-view service per article for those journals and volumes to which you did not subscribe.

Full text is provided in PDF. In order to read these documents you will need Adobe Acrobat Reader, which is freely available from **www.adobe.com/products/ acrobat/readstep2.html**

You can access the electronic edition through the gateways of major subscription agents (SwetsWise, EBSCO EJS, Maruzen) or directly through IngentaConnect.

If you currently use **www.ingenta.com** or **www.ingentaselect.com** (formely, Catchword) to access your subscriptions, these rights have been carried over to **www. ingentaconnect.com**, the new, fully merged service. All bookmarked pages will also be diverted to the relevant pages on **www.ingentaconnect.com**.

If you have not yet set up access to the electronic version of the journal at IngentaConnect, please follow these instructions:

If you are a personal subscriber:
- Register free at **www.ingentaconnect.com**. This is a one-time process, that provides IngentaConnect with the information they need to be able to match your data with the subscription data provide by the publisher. Your registration also allows you to use the e-mail alerting services.
- Select *Personal subscriptions.*
- Select the publication title and enter your subscription number. Your subscription number can be found on the shipping label with the print journal, and on the invoice/renewal invitation.
- You will be notified by email once your online access has been activated.

If you are an institutional subscriber:
- Register free at **www.ingentaconnect.com** by selecting the registration link and following the link to institutional registration.
- Select *Set up subscriptions.*
- Select the publication title and enter your subscription number. Your subscription number can be found on the shipping label with the print journal, and on the invoice/renewal invitation.
- You will be notified by email once your online access has been activated.

If you purchase subscriptions via a subscription agent they will be able to set up subscriptions on IngentaConnect on your behalf – simply pass them your IngentaConnect ID, sent to you at registration.

If you would like further information or assistance with your registration, please contact **help@ingentaconnect.com**.

For information on our journals, please visit **www.benjamins.com**

New in Applied Linguistics

ESP in European Higher Education
Integrating language and content

Edited by Inmaculada Fortanet-Gómez and Christine A. Räisänen

Universitat Jaume I, Castelló / Chalmers University, Gothenburg

The Bologna Reform has been implemented in a large part of the European Union and it is time to take a short pause to reflect over some of the lessons learned up to now. The aim of this book is to share experiences and reflections on English for Specific Purposes pedagogy in Western European higher education. Taking as a starting point the development of the EU policies during the past couple of decades and their national implementations, the chapters in this book provide various perspectives, both theoretical and practical, on the ways in which the reform has been implemented and its effects on the teaching of ESP. Experiences of developing programmes and courses incorporating Content and Language Integrated Learning and Autonomous and Lifelong Learning are described, as well as Problem-Based Learning and Process-Genre Pedagogies. The book also includes chapters on the crucial, but often neglected issue of teacher support in meeting the challenges of teaching content through the medium of English.

[AILA Applied Linguistics Series, 4] 2008. vi, 285 pp.
HB 978 90 272 0520 9 EUR 99.00 / USD 149.00

Dimensions of Forensic Linguistics
Edited by John Gibbons and M. Teresa Turell

University of Western Sydney / Universitat Pompeu Fabra, Barcelona

This volume functions as a guide to the multidisciplinary nature of Forensic Linguistics understood in its broadest sense as the interface between language and the law. It seeks to address the links in this relatively young field between theory, method and data, without neglecting the need for new research questions in the field. Perhaps the most striking feature of this collection is its range, strikingly illustrating the multi-dimensionality of Forensic Linguistics. All of the contributions share a preoccupation with the painstaking linguistic work involved, using and interpreting data in a restrained and reasoned way.

[AILA Applied Linguistics Series, 5] 2008. vi, 316 pp.
HB 978 90 272 0521 6 EUR 99.00 / USD 149.00

For full title information see *www.benjamins.com*

Dictionary Use in Foreign Language Writing Exams

Impact and implications

Martin East

Unitec New Zealand / The University of Auckland

This book provides an in-depth analysis of what happens when
intermediate level learners of a foreign language use a bilingual
dictionary when writing. Dictionaries are frequently promoted to
people learning a foreign language. Nevertheless, teachers often
talk about their students' inability to use dictionaries properly,
especially when they write, and this can be problematic. This book
paints a comprehensive picture of the differences a dictionary
makes and brings out the implications for language learning, teaching, and testing practices.
It draws on research in which participants in three studies took writing tests in two test
conditions – with and without a dictionary. They were also asked what they thought about
the two test types. Their performances and opinions were analyzed in a variety of ways.
Conclusions from the data highlight some of the practical issues to be kept in mind if we
want to help foreign language learners to use bilingual dictionaries effectively when writing.

[Language Learning & Language Teaching, 22] 2008. xiii, 228 pp.

HB   978 90 272 1983 1   EUR 105.00 / USD 158.00

Second Language Acquisition and the Younger Learner

Child's play?

Edited by Jenefer Philp, Rhonda Oliver and Alison Mackey

University of Auckland / Edith Cowan University, Bunbury /
Georgetown University

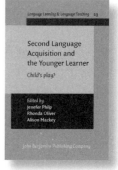

This new volume of work highlights the distinctiveness of
child SLA through a collection of different types of empirical
research specific to younger learners. Characteristics of children's
cognitive, emotional, and social development distinguish
their experiences from those of adult L2 learners, creating
intriguing issues for SLA research, and also raising important practical questions
regarding effective pedagogical techniques for learners of different ages. While child
SLA is often typically thought of as simple (and often enjoyable and universally
effortless), in other words, as "child's play", the complex portraits of young second
language learners which emerge in the 16 papers collected in this book invite the
reader to reconsider the reality for many younger learners. Chapters by internationally
renowned authors together with reports by emerging researchers describe second and
foreign language learning by children ranging from pre-schoolers to young adolescents,
in home and school contexts, with caregivers, peers, and teachers as interlocutors.

[Language Learning & Language Teaching, 23] 2008. viii, 334 pp.

HB   978 90 272 1984 8   EUR 105.00 / USD 158.00
PB   978 90 272 1985 5   EUR 36.00 / USD 54.00

For full title information see *www.benjamins.com*

New in Applied Linguistics

Corpora and Language Teaching

Edited by Karin Aijmer

University of Gothenburg

The articles in this edited volume represent a broad coverage
of areas. They discuss the role and effectiveness of corpora
and corpus-linguistic techniques for language teaching but
also deal with broader issues such as the relationship between
corpora and second language teaching and how the different
perspectives of foreign language teachers and applied linguists
can be reconciled. A number of concrete examples are given of
how authentic corpus material can be used for different learning
activities in the classroom. It is also shown how specific learner problems for example
in the area of phraseology can be studied on the basis of learner corpora and textbook
corpora. On the basis of learner corpora of speech and writing it is further shown that
even advanced learners of English are uncertain about stylistic and text type differences.

[Studies in Corpus Linguistics, 33]   2009.   viii, 232 pp.

HB   978 90 272 2307 4   EUR 99.00 / USD 149.00

Linear Unit Grammar

Integrating speech and writing

John McH. Sinclair and Anna Mauranen

Tuscan Word Centre / University of Helsinki

People have a natural propensity to understand language
text as a succession of smallish chunks, whether they are
reading, writing, speaking or listening. Linguists have
found that this propensity can shed light on the nature and
structure of language, and there are many studies which
attempt to harness the potential of natural chunking.

This book explores the role of chunking in the description of discourse, especially
spoken discourse. It appears that chunking offers a sound but flexible platform on
which can be built a descriptive model which is more open and comprehensive than
more familiar approaches to structural description. The model remains linear, in that
it avoids hierarchies, and it concentrates on the combinatorial patterns of text.

The linear approach turns out to have many advantages, bringing
together under one descriptive method a wide variety of different styles
of speech and writing. It is complementary to established grammars, but
it raises pertinent questions about many of their assumptions.

[Studies in Corpus Linguistics, 25]   2006.   xxii, 185 pp.

HB   978 90 272 2298 5   EUR 95.00 / USD 143.00
PB   978 90 272 2299 2   EUR 33.00 / USD 49.95

For full title information see *www.benjamins.com*

Television Dialogue

The sitcom *Friends* vs. natural conversation

Paulo Quaglio

State University of New York at Cortland

This book explores a virtually untapped, yet fascinating research area: television dialogue. It reports on a study comparing the language of the American situation comedy *Friends* to natural conversation. Transcripts of the television show and the American English conversation portion of the *Longman Grammar Corpus* provide the data for this corpus-based investigation, which combines Douglas Biber's multidimensional methodology with a frequency-based analysis of close to 100 linguistic features. As a natural offshoot of the research design, this study offers a comprehensive description of the most common linguistic features characterizing natural conversation. Illustrated with numerous dialogue extracts from *Friends* and conversation, topics such as vague, emotional, and informal language are discussed. This book will be an important resource not only for researchers and students specializing in discourse analysis, register variation, and corpus linguistics, but also anyone interested in conversational language and television dialogue.

[Studies in Corpus Linguistics, 36] 2009. xiii, 165 pp

HB   978 90 272 2310 4 EUR 95.00 / USD 143.00

ConcGram 1.0

A phraseological search engine

Chris Greaves

The Hong Kong Polytechnic University

ConcGram 1.0 is a corpus linguistics software package which is specifically designed to find all the co-occurrences of words in a text or corpus irrespective of variation. The software finds the co-occurrences fully automatically, in other words, the user inputs no prior search commands. These co-occurrences are termed 'concgrams' and include instances of both constituency variation (*increase* in *expenditure*, *increase* in the share of public *expenditure*) and positional variation (*expenditure* would inevitably *increase*). ConcGram 1.0 is therefore uniquely suited to uncovering the full phraseological profile of a text or corpus. In addition to this principal function, ConcGram 1.0 allows the user to nominate concgram searches, and it also has the more traditional functions associated with corpus linguistics software.

The software comes with a detailed online manual in a PDF file, which explains all of the functions and includes a user-friendly tutorial. In addition, the manual includes a discussion of the theoretical issues underpinning the development of the software and the implications of concgramming for the study of phraseology (*Why Concgram?* by Martin Warren).

The software has a wide range of applications in the fields of Corpus Linguistics, Critical Discourse Analysis, Discourse Analysis, Lexicology, Lexicography, Pragmatics and Semantics.

[Studies in Corpus Linguistics Software, 1] 2009.

CD   978 90 272 4027 9 PRICE TO BE ANNOUNCED

Expected April 2009

For full title information see *www.benjamins.com*